Compliance-Industrial Complex

Tereza Østbø Kuldova

Compliance-Industrial Complex

The Operating System of a Pre-Crime Society

Tereza Østbø Kuldova
Work Research Institute
Oslo Metropolitan University
Oslo, Norway

ISBN 978-3-031-19223-4   ISBN 978-3-031-19224-1   (eBook)
https://doi.org/10.1007/978-3-031-19224-1

This Palgrave Macmillan imprint is published by the registered company Springer Nature Switzerland AG
The registered company address is: Gewerbestrasse 11, 6330 Cham, Switzerland

PREFACE

Politics is dead. Meet compliance, the new Leviathan, the Franken-
stein built to eradicate all evil. Enter the world of regulations, directives, standards, guidelines, and codes of conduct and ethics. Enter the
world of experts who translate policies that aim to fight corruption,
money laundering, financial crimes, human rights abuses, and more,
into technobureaucratic compliance systems, integrity training and algorithmic monitoring and surveillance systems. Meet the multi-billion-dollar
industry to which states have delegated the authority and power to collect
intelligence, investigate, and manufacture suspicion—and to govern us, in
the name of the undisputable *good*, in the name of the elimination of all
the things we all can agree are evil. Excited by yet another regulation of
yet another societal evil, by yet another 'move in the right direction', we
rarely pause to think about what kind of world these anti-policies that
target crimes, security threats, risks, and harms, are creating. This book,
an essay in two parts, sets out to change this. Next time you read in
the news of a new regulation being implemented, you will think of the
markets that crop up in its wake, and about the powers that those who are
meant to comply with it, paradoxically, acquire; about how the regulation
may be translated into practice, or even abused. And you will think about
the consequences this may have for justice, democracy, and freedom of
speech. Next time, you will pause before asking for *more* of the same
regulatory solutions.

This essay unpacks what I call the 'compliance-industrial complex', a transversal social phenomenon which has so far managed to blossom below the academic radar. Rather than offering a definitive take, or an in-depth empirical account, this essay aims first and foremost to find the right concepts that can help us understand and lure this monster out in the light. The compliance-industrial complex has so far not been dealt with as a phenomenon in its own right, despite the fact that it is accumulating power and wealth from the way we have chosen to govern our societies, as we speak. And despite the fact that it is essential in the reproduction and legitimization of corporate power. The compliance-industrial complex translates noble ideas into practices of control and pre-emption of future risks, into new forms of hybrid policing; it shapes the ways in which we are governed, profiled, sorted, surveilled, nudged, risk-assessed, punished, sanctioned—as workers, clients, customers, suppliers, and humans. Compliance, as I argue, is fast becoming a new logic of governance, supported by the apparatuses of corporate security and private intelligence. This logic is being built into algorithmic management systems, into data-driven predictive tools, into various technologies that seek to control and predict our behaviours and emotions, into technologies that are unable to see us otherwise than as (potential) crime and security threats, as impostors or fakes, and as suspects. Compliance, as I try to show, is likely to enhance corporate sovereignty and corporate power, while imposing a new broader regime of power and control. Supported by advances in artificial intelligence (AI), it is quickly becoming the operating system of a pre-crime society, reshaping subjectivities and interpellating individuals as ideological subjects in new ways. How can we challenge the operating system itself?

The book draws on a number of traditions, in particular anthropology, critical criminology and critical algorithm studies to disrupt the established and narrow discourses on compliance, which has largely been treated within the frameworks of business management, corporate governance, law, and accounting, with very few and limited criminological contributions. This literature typically tends to focus on policy issues and regulatory requirements, remaining firmly trapped in state-centric perspectives, often ignoring regulatory blurring and hybridization and the role of the private sector in governance, which are central to this book. When the reality on the ground is one of progressive hybridization and blurring, it also becomes impossible to remain constrained by disciplinary boundaries and highly specialized research questions. To the contrary, it becomes imperative to find new ways of speaking about this world and grasping it in its complexity. This specialization has, in my view, prevented us from adequately naming and conceptualizing the phenomenon which is right in front of us, and which increasingly shapes our everyday lives. Hence, I argue that the compliance-industrial complex needs to be analysed as a socio-political and economic phenomenon, as a market in expertise that is instrumental to the pluralization and privatization of policing. Private intelligence, private security, and big tech companies are increasingly concentrated at the very core of compliance and at the core of the governance of the social. A picture of securitized and criminalized compliance as a mode of governance emerges, of governance that increasingly relies on intelligence-led and predictive technologies to control future risks, crimes, and security threats, both real and imaginary. Alas, recognizing it as such becomes even harder when it takes the shape of a largely invisibilized, highly technical and expert and data-driven infrastructure, an operating system we either fail to notice— the same way the fish don't know they are in water—or disavow. While some critics focus on this or that app, this or that technology, this or that regulation, this book tries to grasp the underlying logic of this operating system rather than targeting its multiple manifestations. This is not to say that it is not interesting or important to see how matters play out in specific contexts, but simply that this is not the aim of this book. Indeed, in order to grasp such a transversal phenomenon, some detail must necessarily be sacrificed. Only by sacrificing the technical details we can ask the fundamental questions.

This book is divided into two parts. In the first part of this essay, I introduce the concept of the *compliance-industrial complex*, the power complex at the intersection of the regulatory state and corporate capital, comprising diverse and often networked actors: governmental officials, civil servants, and bureaucrats, lawmakers, regulators, law enforcement and intelligence services, lobbyists, NGOs, standardization bodies, audit, consultancy, and tech companies in the growing business of ensuring regulatory compliance and translating regulation into services and products. I show how this multi-billion-dollar industry has emerged in response to and depends on the proliferation of regulation and *anti-policies* that combat all sorts of evils and that it is impossible to be *against*: especially in the fields of anti-corruption, anti-money laundering (AML), and combatting the financing of terrorism (CFT). Simultaneously, more and more regulatory concerns that take the form of anti-policies have been and are being incorporated into the compliance logic of the anti-corruption/AML architecture: from sanctions regimes to human rights, anti-radicalization or forced labour, and environmental due diligence. This anti-policy syndrome has stimulated the growth of the compliance-industrial complex. But the compliance-industrial complex, I argue, is not only fuelled by the convergence of particular anti-policy regulatory visions—public and private, but also by industry promises of fighting corruption, financial crime, terrorism financing, and a host of other global crime issues from integrated *platforms* and through the same *logic* of *risk management* and anticipatory and predictive *pre-crime* governance, relying on surveillance, monitoring, and risk modelling. In the compliance-industrial complex, 'regulatory capitalism' (Levi-Faur, 2017) and 'surveillance capitalism' (Zuboff, 2019) converge. The intensions of anti-policies and of the global fight against crime may be noble, but it is high time that we ask what we are actually *for* when we embrace the solutions on offer. The first part of this essay thus opens the argument that runs through this book, namely that the compliance-industrial complex is increasingly becoming an operating system of a *pre-crime* society (Arrigo & Sellers, 2021), an often invisibilized infrastructure, a form of opaque 'extrastatecraft' (Easterling, 2016), one, paradoxically, driven by visions of transparency and accountability. It leads the reader step by step towards the argument that the compliance-industrial complex is increasingly shaping the ways in which we are governed, controlled, surveilled, nudged, risk-assessed, punished, sanctioned, sorted, and even understood as humans. It sounds a note of caution that when we stand united behind good-intentioned policies that promise to combat all sorts of evils and all the things that nobody in their right mind can be for, we may both blind ourselves to the ways in which they are being translated into practice and to the ways in which they are reshaping the very fabric of social life. We may ignore their criminogenic effects, their inefficiencies, the role they play in entrenching inequalities, new injustices, and harms, or in further empowering the already powerful. And we may ignore the ways in which they entrench the logic of policing and intelligence gathering into the everyday, and with it the logic of suspicion, thus naturalizing the emergence of a post-political/apolitical *pre-crime* society.

The second part of the book looks more closely at the forms of knowledge(-production) that underpin compliance as well as the professionalization of compliance, and the ways in which both align themselves with the trends we see in the data-driven predictive and platform policing

(Ferguson, 2017; Wilson, 2019). These forms of knowledge, the experts, and professionals, along with standards, best practice guidelines, and codes of conduct, inform not only organizational practices but also the algorithmic architectures that subject, subjectify, and interpellate employees, clients, consumers, suppliers, and others. I show how the algorithmic architectures of RegTech and of the compliance-industrial complex at large are being integrated into performance management, insider threat management systems, as well as corporate security infrastructures and other feats of techno-social managerial engineering taking on punitive roles. These compliance technologies tend to create hostile algorithmic environments of control that aim to manage, police, track, influence, nudge, and predict not only behaviours, motivations, emotions, and actions, but also the unconscious. It is here that we see the links between large structures, organizational life, and subjectivity, between macro- and micro-sociology, unfold. Refracted through the lenses of RegTech and various applications of data-driven solutions to prevent crime, fraud, misconduct, and internal and external security threats, the corporate enforcement and management of 'compliance culture' and of ethics increasingly take the shape of predictive and intelligence-led policing, resulting in both sanctions and 'pre-punishment' (Zedner, 2007). As compliance, risk, and human resource management fuse with these platform infrastructures, they increasingly seek to 'govern the soul' (Rose, 1999) of workers and others, and to make it 'legible' (Scott, 1998) to the corporate gaze. What does seeing like a corporate sovereign mean when this pre-crime 'governance of the soul' merges with different forms of post-political and technobureaucratic 'algorithmic governance' (Kalpokas, 2019; Katzenbach & Ulbricht, 2019), turning into a form of 'extrastatecraft' (Easterling, 2016)? What does it mean to become (a) subject to the corporate sovereign?

Oslo, Norway   Tereza Østbø Kuldova

References

Arrigo, B., & Sellers, B. (Eds.). (2021). *The Pre-crime society: Crime, culture and control in the ultramodern age.* Bristol University Press. https://doi.org/10.1332/policypress/9781529205251.001.0001

Easterling, K. (2016). *Extrastatecraft: The power of infrastructure space.* Verso.

Ferguson, A. G. (2017). *The rise of big data policing: Surveillance, race, and the future of law enforcement.* New York University Press. https://doi.org/10.2307/j.ctt1pwtb27

Kalpokas, I. (2019). *Algorithmic governance: Politics and law in the post-human era.* Palgrave Macmillan. https://doi.org/10.1007/978-3-030-31922-9

Katzenbach, C., & Ulbricht, L. (2019). Algorithmic governance. *Internet Policy Review, 8*(4), 1–18. https://doi.org/10.14763/2019.4.1424

Levi-Faur, D. (2017). Regulatory capitalism. In P. Drahos (Ed.), *Regulatory theory: Foundation and applications* (pp. 289–302). ANU Press. https://doi.org/10.22459/RT.02.2017.17

Rose, N. (1999). *Governing the soul: The shaping of the private self.* Free Association Books.

Scott, J. C. (1998). *Seeing like a state: How certain schemes to improve the human condition have failed.* Yale University Press.

Wilson, D. (2019). Platform policing and the real-time cop. *Surveillance & Society, 17*(1), 69–75. https://doi.org/10.24908/ss.v17i1/2.12958

Zedner, L. (2007). Preventive justice or pre-punishment? The case of control orders. *Current Legal Problems, 60*(1), 174–203. https://doi.org/10.1093/clp/60.1.174

Zuboff, S. (2019). *The age of surveillance capitalism: The fight for a human future at the new frontier of power.* Profile Books.

ACKNOWLEDGEMENTS

This short book springs from synergies between two ongoing international research projects funded by the Research Council of Norway. The first project *Luxury, Corruption and Global Ethics: Towards a Critical Cultural Theory of the Moral Economy of Fraud (LUXCORE) [project no. 313004]*, which I lead, investigates the global governance of corruption and the dynamics between compliance and defiance. The second project *Algorithmic Governance and Cultures of Policing: Comparative Perspectives from Norway, India, Brazil, Russia, and South Africa (AGOPOL) [project no. 313626]*, which I co-lead, investigates the logic of predictive and intelligence-led policing in different cultural settings, and where policing is understood as increasingly privatized and pluralized. This book is a result of ethnographic fieldwork among compliance professionals, extensive policy document analysis, and expert interviews conducted as part of our research project on corruption, but the insights gained into the industry and its logic would not have been possible without the extensive research on algorithmic governance, and privatization and pluralization of policing in a data-driven world, which have brought me to my inquiries into regulatory technologies (RegTech). I would like to thank all my colleagues engaged in these two projects for all the inspiring conversations, special thanks go to Jardar Østbø, Bitten Nordrik, Thomas Raymen, Davide Casciano, Petr Kupka, Steve Hall, Christin Thea Wathne, Helene O. I. Gundhus, Joanne Roberts, Cris Shore, Shivangi Narayan, Tomas Salem, Ella Paneyakh, Dean Wilson,

Ursula Rao, Paulo Cruz Terra, Kjetil Klette Bøhler, Veronika Nagy, Eivind Falkum, Anthony Lloyd, Kristin Reichborn-Kjennerud, Ingrid M. Tolstad, Aleksandra Bartoszko, Simon Winlow, Lill-Ann Chepstow-Lusty, Daniel Briggs, and the Research Council of Norway for enabling and supporting this research and lasting collaborations. This book has also greatly benefited from the discussions with the members of the *Algorithmic Governance Research Network*, which I have established in 2020, and from the conversations with authors which I have hosted at my podcast channel, *Black Box by Algorithmic Governance Research Network*. Moreover, this book has benefitted from many years of conversations and encounters with numerous brilliant colleagues from across anthropology and critical and ultra-realist criminology, and from my editorial work in the *Journal of Extreme Anthropology* which I have established and where I serve as the editor-in-chief, the authors contributing to this journal serve as an endless source of inspiration.

CONTENTS

Part I   Compliance-Industrial Complex and the Anti-Policy Syndrome

1   **Introduction to Part I: Compliance-Industrial Complex and the Anti-policy Syndrome**   3
    References   17

2   **The Anti-policy Syndrome**   21
    On the Expanding Risk Universe   23
    On Standing (Morally) United Against ... a Threat to Our Security   28
    On Technosolutionism   31
    On Regulatory Hybridization and Blurring   35
    References   41

3   **The Compliance-Industrial Complex**   47
    On Scandals   49
    On the Shift from Legal Compliance to Ethical Compliance Cultures   51
    On Compliance as Pre-Emptive Intelligence-Led Governance   54
    On Intelligence-Led Compliance as a Route to Corporate Sovereignty   56
    Why Bother About the Compliance-Industrial Complex?   60
    References   66

**Part II   Compliance as the Operating System of a
Pre-Crime Society**

**4   Introduction to Part II: Compliance as the Operating
System of a Pre-Crime Society**   73
References   78

5   The Pre-emption of Dissent   81
*On the Enlisting of the Whistleblower in the Service
of Intelligence*   83
*On the Shift from Whistleblower Protection to Threat
Management*   87
*On Ensuring Compliance Through Pre-Crime
and Corporate Security*   90
References   94

6   Compliance-Industrial Complex and Its Experts   97
On the Struggle for Professional Legitimacy   100
On ISO Standards and the Manufacturing of Consensus   104
On the Failures that Stimulate the Quest for More of the Same   108
References   111

**7   Artificial Intelligence, Algorithmic Governance,
and the Manufacturing of Suspicion and Risk**   115
On the (Suspect) Promises of Artificial Intelligence   118
On RegTech and Algorithmic Governance   129
On the Operating System of a Pre-Crime Society   133
References   145

Epilogue   153

Index   161

ABOUT THE AUTHOR

Tereza Østbø Kuldova is a Research Professor at the Work Research Institute, OsloMet—Oslo Metropolitan University, Norway. She holds a Ph.D. in social anthropology from the University of Oslo (2013) and is the author of *How Outlaws Win Friends and Influence People* (Palgrave, 2019), *Luxury Indian Fashion: A Social Critique* (Bloomsbury, 2016), co-editor of *Crime, Harm and Consumerism* (Routledge, 2020), *Outlaw Motorcycle Clubs and Street Gangs* (Palgrave, 2018), and *Urban Utopias: Excess and Expulsion in Neoliberal South Asia* (Palgrave, 2017). She has published numerous articles in journals such as *Trends in Organized Crime, Visual Anthropology, Journal of Design History, Cultural Politics*, and more and contributed chapters to edited volumes. She has written on subjects as diverse as philanthrocapitalism, Indian luxury fashion industry, intellectual property rights, organized crime, outlaw motorcycle clubs, and more. Her latest monograph in Norwegian, co-authored with Bitten Nordrik, dealt with investigative methods in Norwegian workplaces *Faktaundersøkelser: et 'hybrid konfliktvåpen' på norske arbeidsplasser (Fact-finding Investigations: A 'Hybrid Conflict Weapon' in Norwegian Workplaces*, Gyldendal Akademisk, 2021). Currently, she works on the intersection of algorithmic and global governance, surveillance, and artificial intelligence, organized white-collar crime and corruption, the compliance industry, and the pluralization of policing as well as worker monitoring and labour rights. She is the founder and editor-in-chief of the *Journal of Extreme Anthropology* and of the *Algorithmic Governance Research Network*.

ABBREVIATIONS

AI	Artificial Intelligence
AML	Anti-Money Laundering
CFT	Combating the Financing of Terrorism
CPE	Continuous Professional Education
CSR	Corporate Social Responsibility
DOJ	Department of Justice, US
EDD	Enhanced Due Diligence
ESG	Environmental, Social, and Governance
FATF	Financial Action Task Force
FCPA	Foreign Corrupt Practices Act, US
FIU	Financial Intelligence Unit
HRM	Human Resource Management
HUMINT	Human Intelligence
IAF	International Accreditation Forum
IMF	International Monetary Fund
INSA	Intelligence and National Security Alliance
ISO	International Organization for Standardization
KYC	Know Your Customer
NGO	Non-Governmental Organization
NPM	New Public Management
OECD	Organization for Economic Cooperation and Development
OFAC	Office of Foreign Assets Control, US
OSINT	Open-Source Intelligence
RegTech	Regulatory Technologies
SAR	Suspicious Activity Report
SDG	Sustainable Development Goals

SupTech	Supervisory Technologies
UN	United Nations
UNDOC	United Nations Office on Drugs and Crime
USDT	United States Department of the Treasury

PART I

Compliance-Industrial Complex and the Anti-Policy Syndrome

Introduction to Part I: Compliance-Industrial Complex and the Anti-policy Syndrome

Abstract This chapter takes as a starting point the *United States Strategy on Countering Corruption* released by the Biden-Harris Administration in December 2021, introducing the reader to the logic of anti-policies, which stimulate the growth of the compliance-industrial complex. We touch upon the intertwined processes of securitization and promulgation of techno-social engineering, risk management, and anticipatory governance. We consider how regulations impose both legal and moral obligations onto organizations and how these become subsumed under the logic of compliance, which is perpetually refining, fine-tuning, optimizing, and building the technobureaucratic control, risk, and surveillance architectures in the name of regulatory compliance and the 'good' and 'ethical'. We open the question of what kind of society these anti-policies that seek to pre-empt all possible evils are creating.

Keywords Anti-corruption · Anti-money laundering (AML) · Securitization · Compliance · Technobureaucracy

Following Joe Biden's *National Security Study Memorandum/NSSM-1* released on June 3, 2021, the fight against corruption was established as a 'core United States national security interest'.[1] Corruption has been, yet again, framed in the familiar tropes as the 'cancer within the body of societies—a disease that eats at public trust and the ability of governments to deliver for their citizens',[2] both a cause and a symptom of a broad spectre of global harms: ineffective governance, market distortion, rising inequality, extremism, migration, economic slowdown, plummeting trust in governments, misappropriation of public assets, illicit financial flows, organized crime, authoritarianism, and more. Again, corruption has been designated as *the* evil to be combatted and eradicated (Underkuffler, 2013), but this time, in addition to the moral, political, symbolic, and economic importance of the fight against corruption for the Western liberal order set on imposing its standards of good governance, transparency, and accountability on the rest of the world, corruption has been for the first time also officially upgraded to a matter of *national security*. Or as Biden put it,

> corruption threatens United States national security, economic equity, global anti-poverty and development efforts, and democracy itself. By effectively preventing and countering corruption and demonstrating the advantages of transparent and accountable governance, we can secure a critical advantage for the United States and other democracies.[3]

The *United States Strategy on Countering Corruption*,[4] which was consequently launched in December 2021, was widely deemed as both aggressive and ambitious—a consolidation of the global governance efforts across the past decades in the field. It promised an *intensification* of both national and global enforcement of anti-corruption, anti-bribery, and anti-money laundering (AML) measures in years to come. But it also *securitized* the fight against corruption; it framed corruption as a legitimate security problem, as a threat, and as an extraordinary issue outside of

[1] https://irp.fas.org/offdocs/nsm/nssm-1.pdf (last accessed January 31, 2022), p. 2.

[2] https://www.whitehouse.gov/briefing-room/statements-releases/2021/12/06/fact-sheet-u-s-strategy-on-countering-corruption/ (last accessed January 31, 2022).

[3] https://irp.fas.org/offdocs/nsm/nssm-1.pdf (last accessed January 31, 2022; emphasis mine), p. 1.

[4] https://www.whitehouse.gov/wp-content/uploads/2021/12/United-States-Strategy-on-Countering-Corruption.pdf (last accessed January 31, 2022).

the realm of normal politics, passing into the extrapolitical realm of emergency, thus demanding exceptional treatment (Buzan et al., 1998). In many ways, this move towards securitization is not unique. Anti-policies that fight this or that unwanted phenomenon proliferate—be they in the form of multilateral treaties and international conventions, national regulations and acts, or corporate policies and codes of conduct. While they may target corruption, human rights abuses, or sexual harassment, they tend to frame criminal offences along with other acts deemed immoral or anti-social in one way or another, in terms of security. This 'securitization of society' has resulted not only in the proliferation of 'quasi-criminal law' (Schuilenburg, 2011), but also in the growth of non-state security, intelligence, consultancy, and other actors selling prevention, security, risk management, and other products that promise to control futures. Securitization for obvious reasons demands a shift towards *anticipatory* forms of governance; towards prediction, pre-emption, and 'pre-crime'; or else, towards the elimination of the unwanted *before* it occurs. With the rise of big data analytics and machine learning, these promises have taken a predominantly data-driven turn. We imagine that social, political, and economic problems can be solved through technical fixes, through more data, better predictions, and more transparency, which would, almost magically, translate into more integrity and more accountability. Securitization thus aligns well with the shift away from 'government' to 'governance by numbers' and to a 'cybernetic imaginary' that 'enacts the dream of an arithmetically attainable social harmony', producing an 'idea of normativity not as legislation but as programming', where 'people are no longer expected to act freely within the limits laid down by the law, but to react in real time to the multiple signals they receive' (Supiot, 2017, p. 10). Or else, it aligns well with the imaginary of humans as *programmable*, of a world where 'techno-social engineering' (Frischmann & Selinger, 2018) and where algorithmic architectures that nudge the optimizable humans into beneficial directions, replace politics. The *United States Strategy on Countering Corruption* reflects both this imaginary and the currently *hegemonic* 'policy framing' and discourse (Bacchi, 2000) of anti-corruption, and other related increasingly securitized anti-policies. The strategy is emblematic of the ways in which Western societies have chosen to frame and tackle pressing global crime and security issues—namely, as to a large degree a *technobureaucratic* matter of compliance, risk and threat management, accounting, auditing, intelligence gathering, and reporting.

These anti-policies are of interest for us insofar as they stimulate the growth of the compliance industry and of so-called RegTech, or regulatory technologies; they place *legal and moral obligations* on the private sector, and even public bodies to engage in internal policing and intelligence gathering for the state and in the name of combatting diverse security threats; obligations with which they need to comply, but that also empower them in ways that may result in the creation of a precrime society. The compliance function, which is now *the* corporate response to the diverse anti-policy regimes, emerged in response to the United States model of corporate criminal liability which 'strives to induce corporate policing by offering settlements without criminal convictions' (Arlen & Buell, 2020, p. 702), and which holds corporations 'criminally liable for any crime committed by any employee in the scope of employment' (Arlen & Buell, 2020, p. 700). Within this model of corporate policing, 'employees face a substantially higher threat of punishment when corporations have strong incentives to detect misconduct, report it, investigate it, and provide actionable evidence to government officials about individual wrongdoers' (Arlen & Buell, 2020, p. 702). The large high-profile settlements in the United States and the threat of spectacular enforcement actions, still unique in the global context, have made the motive for corporate policing only stronger. With globalization, with the shift towards the logic of pre-crime, prediction, and prevention embedded in anti-policies and in anticipatory risk management, and with the increased power of transnational audit and consulting firms, compliance has spread through 'best practice' guidelines, standards, voluntary self-regulation and so on, to organizations, public and private, across the globe, becoming a popular form of governance. While there are important legal differences between different jurisdictions and growing legal debate about compliance, our aim here is to shed light on compliance as a transversal social phenomenon and governance logic which is gaining traction globally, legitimized by the legal and moral obligations imposed *through* and by anti-policy regimes.

This short book, or rather an essay in two parts, aims to think the possible consequences of the ways in which we have chosen to govern global crime and other phenomena that become refracted through the same lens of crime and security. What kind of a society are we creating when criminalized and securitized technobureaucratic compliance becomes *the* go to mode of governance of the social? The number of private partners being enlisted in the global fight against crime is growing, and so is their power to shape the very regulations to which they are to submit and comply with; they are de facto delegating these 'policing' powers to themselves while partaking in the power of the state. These powers can then be used to monitor, surveil, sort, risk assess, control, and sanction workers, suppliers, clients, consumers, citizens through technobureaucratic, administrative, and (semi)automated processes. These extrajudicial processes are not only extremely difficult to challenge, but also tend to reproduce and reinforce structural inequalities and relations of power. As the securitization of society progresses, at the level of organizations, management becomes compliance and vice versa, and compliance a form of data-driven predictive policing which becomes in many ways ubiquitous, built into both the algorithmic and physical infrastructures of our everyday life—in the name of the good and the elimination of the negative.

The ruthless focus on revenue and shareholder capitalism, we are told, has been replaced by 'stakeholder capitalism', 'ethical capitalism', by 'business for good', by socially and environmentally conscious ways of doing business and investing, and by 'philanthrocapitalism' (McGoey, 2012) and so on. This 'capitalism with a human face' (Žižek, 2009) is posited, in the manner of 'capitalist realism' (Fisher, 2009) as the only thinkable way of life, the only way to deliver solutions to our problems. Anti-policies are well aligned with this mode of thinking and typically see solutions in different ways of regulating and nudging business for the good, enlisting business as a partner in crime fighting first and a regulated entity second. The formerly vague promises and initiatives of business ethics and corporate social responsibility (CSR) and other forms of self-regulation and soft law have been progressively transformed and built into more and more detailed regulations by states and international regulatory bodies. The move towards what some have called the 'regulatory state' (Grabosky, 2013; Veggeland, 2009), or even 'regulatory capitalism' (Braithwaite, 2008; Levi-Faur, 2005, 2017), has thus been happening parallel with the proclaimed shift towards 'business for good'. It is in this context that phenomena such as corruption became reframed and refracted through the lens of corporate governance, in particular as implemented by regulated entities, such as banks or the finance sector, which tend to set the tone and others emulate (Sampson, 2021). It is here that a vast industry has emerged catering to the need for regulatory compliance, while championing the 'ethical turn'; from mere compliance officers, we have now moved to chief compliance *and* ethics officers who team up with HR and other managerial functions. The turn from development economics to ethics in anti-corruption is also visible in the proliferation of new benchmarks and indicators of ethical compliance and ethical culture, in the growth of integrity management, ethical audit programs, and proliferation of ethical trainings as part of anti-corruption compliance and training programs, or for that matter in OECD's Public Integrity Indicators.[5] Or as Diligent puts it in their '10 Traits of a Strong Culture of Compliance':

> The keys to success are clear policies, strong procedures, and unshakable core ethical values — so that employees want to pursue ethical conduct, and have a clear path to do so in their daily routines. That's what regulators want to see: a culture of compliance that exists irrespective of any single person's commitment to ethics and compliance.[6]

The compliance industry, I argue, has found its niche in perpetually refining, fine-tuning, optimizing, and building the technobureaucratic control, risk, and surveillance architectures in the name of the 'good', the 'ethical', *and* regulatory compliance, becoming the very shapers of the infrastructure of this 'capitalism with a human face'. In the process, it tends to reframe crime, be it corruption, money laundering, terrorism financing, etc., as well as unethical behaviours as matters of both security and reputation best handled by a combination of data-driven risk management and building of 'ethical cultures'. Or as PwC puts it in its promotional e-book 'How Technology Can Power Proactive Risk Management':

> A robust risk management program can play a central role in deepening stakeholder trust. Additionally, the law and culture at large are demanding higher standards in the risk management space. To answer these demands, companies can implement intelligent tech to get ahead of risks before they cause reputational, financial or societal harm. (...) Proactive risk management is good for the business and good for society because it fights crime and reinforces ethical business practices through prevention. (...) In superhero films, we want the good guys to vanquish the villains and keep the world safe from disaster. Employing the right risk management solutions

[5] https://oecd-public-integrity-indicators.org/ (last accessed August 2, 2022).

[6] https://www.diligent.com/-/media/project/diligent/master/insights/white-papers/pdf-media-files/diligentwhitepaper-10-traits-strong-culture.pdf (last accessed August 2, 2022), p. 4.

and approaches can help you become the vanquishing hero in a world increasingly populated by new and different villains engaged in money laundering, cybercrime, corruption or other illegal activity. Technology can become your superpower in this quest.[7]

(Corporate) values and ethical imperatives declared in the various anti-policies are securitized through different forms of internal policing and prosecution of non-compliance, often also at least partially delegated to automated systems. The process of 'securitization of spiritual-moral values', as analysed in the case of the Russian National Security Strategy, is thus not something reserved to the Russian Other, but something that finds its parallels across Western governance and corporate discourses (Østbø, 2017); even if the actual values that are being securitized are indeed different.

Partaking in the securitization of anti-corruption and being enlisted in the fight against global crimes, and even immoral conduct, equip the compliance industry with the powers of largely invisibilized 'extrastate-craft' (Easterling, 2016), a power to govern through the shaping of infrastructures, be these bureaucratic, managerial, procedural, algorithmic, or physical that permit certain actions while prohibiting others and that increasingly define the 'values' and 'ethics' we are to live (=comply) by—the fighting of evil and the deliverance of the 'good' become translated into a matter of internal control architectures, data-driven platforms churning out risk analytics, of 'good governance' procedures, imperatives and (typically empty) principles, codes of conduct, guidelines, and standards to be followed and implemented, or just simply a matter of accounting and audit. In the process, deeply political questions become reduced to matters of technobureaucratic *expertise* requiring specialized detailed knowledge of ethics experts, compliance experts, lawyers, auditors, accountants, security personnel, intelligence officers and so forth, excluding the many from decision-making and from determining which questions can be legitimately asked and which are deemed absurd within the 'technostrategic' discourse (Cohn, 1987). As a rule, it is the principled, fundamental questions that are excluded. It is time to contemplate this particular dark side of 'capitalism with a human face', not necessarily

---

[7] https://images.products.pwc.com/Web/PwCNV/%7B776cebc7-fa37-4541-80d9-a7efa604e453%7DFlagshippiece-Howtechnologycanenableproactiveriskmanagement.pdf (last accessed August 2, 2022), pp. 3, 6.

by looking directly at the exploitation, exacerbation of inequalities, and other harms, as others have done (Glasbeek, 2018; Woodiwiss, 2005), but by looking at the immense power of compliance and 'regulocracy' (Sataøen, 2018) that covers up this exploitation and other harms in layer upon layer of sleek reporting and accounting, and that in the name of transparency obscures these fundamental realities on the ground, while becoming an immense power apparatus in its own right.

This book is neither a treatise in legal studies, nor a classical anthropological or criminological work, despite hovering in between or rather across the latter two disciplines. It is more of a reflexive essay, inspired by the ethnographic fieldwork I conducted both online and offline, and by interviews with informants in the compliance universe, by extensive reading of policy documents as well as academic literature, as well as by previous research on whistleblowing and Kafkaesque workplace and internal investigations executed in the name of *anti*-harassment and breaches of codes of ethics (Kuldova & Nordrik, forthcoming; Nordrik & Kuldova, 2021). This reflexive and transdisciplinary (rather than interdisciplinary) orientation reflects the need to utilize sociological and ethnographic imagination (Mills, 2000; Willis, 2000) to capture the social phenomenon of compliance and the 'transversal' social practices that proliferate within what I term the compliance-industrial complex. Hager Ben Jaffel and Sebastian Larsson have convincingly argued for a similar approach when it comes to the new practices of *intelligence*, which 'has diversified and become increasingly connected to, and understood as, surveillance, policing, counter-terrorism, population management, border checks, communications monitoring, and more' (Ben Jaffel & Larsson, 2022, p. 4) and as

> the specializations and dispositions of those who "do" intelligence have multiplied and shifted from spies and military strategists to police officers, data analysts, IT and communications specialists, border guards, and others. In addition, more and more "unprofessionals of security" (Ragazzi, 2017) – be they ordinary citizens, nurses or teachers – are now increasingly obliged to become actors of intelligence themselves by, for instance, reporting "unusual" behaviour or incidents (Petersen & Tjalve, 2013). (Ben Jaffel & Larsson, 2022, p. 5)

In a similar vein to which even the so-called critical intelligence studies have been unable to address the larger social transformation of intelligence as a social phenomenon, critical management studies, critical criminology, or anthropology have so far been unable to address the transversal phenomenon of compliance. While different aspects of the phenomenon have been discussed, there has not been an effort to make sense of the compliance industry *as* a transversal phenomenon, taking shape in an increasingly complex, blurred, and hybridized reality of securitized, privatized, and pluralized governance and *management* of crime in the context of 'surveillance capitalism' (Zuboff, 2019) and 'audit society' (Power, 1997; Shore & Wright, 2015). Compliance professionals are prominent among the new 'unprofessionals of security' (Ragazzi, 2017), together with data analysts, HR managers, consultants, and others who devise and implement compliance systems. When the world becomes perceived primarily through the lens of risk and security, intelligence work spills rapidly from the imaginary bounds of nation-state security and foreign relations to every nook and corner of society. The notorious 'intelligence cycle' is now part of standard training of compliance officers and anti-money laundering experts, while reporting suspicion and supporting this suspicion by 'intelligence' becomes a normalized managerial practice. In the second part of this essay, the overlaps between intelligence and compliance will come into sharper focus. This essay is therefore also a modest contribution to the project establishing a new research agenda on contemporary intelligence (Ben Jaffel & Larsson, 2022).

Between 2020 and 2022, I have attended over 60 compliance conferences, webinars, and RegTech product presentations—following the idea and methodology of doing ethnographic fieldwork at conferences (Nyquist & Leivestad, 2017); I have also interviewed 20 compliance officers, experts in financial crime, and whistleblowers, in addition to many informal conversations at events; and I have also completed 13 courses in compliance, AML, ISO standardization, anti-corruption of varying quality and cost, and 1 certification in compliance. I have stepped into this terrain as an anthropologist into a foreign culture and uncovered a world of its own, one that some years ago I did not even know existed but that appeared self-evident and the only possible to those inhabiting it: a global culture of compliance professionals and self-proclaimed corporate crime fighters, where the same governance mantras are recited and seem the most natural way to manage the world with little concern for local differences and cultures (with the possible exception of local laws and regulations), a world where the same certificates are coveted and their achievement flaunted in LinkedIn groups, where corporate messaging is applauded and 'hearted', where regulatory handbooks by consulting and legal firms are devoured with appetite, where a never-ceasing flow of webinar invitations keeps reminding you to keep up with the turbulent developments in the global regulatory field while promising to deliver the needed up-to-date knowledge (that, too, is bound to age rapidly), a world where new regulations are met with excitement as they both signify 'progress' and as they demand updating of best practices and ever new solutions to sell to remain compliant, a world where talking of 'measuring compliance culture', of the 'risk universe', of 'insider threats', of one's favourite 'compliance bible' or calling oneself 'fraud fighter', 'compliance evangelist', or 'ethics warrior' is the most natural thing to do, where compliance podcasts are absorbed with the caffeine in the morning cup, but also a world where cynicism often lurks behind the performative staging of excitement about doing good and being compliant. The aim here is not to describe this world in great detail, but rather to capture its inner logic and its power—that which it sees as self-evident, that which it does not question, the metaphors it lives by. To belong to this world in many ways means precisely that one complies with and does not challenge what is deemed 'best practice' at any given moment in the industry, that one celebrates the arrival of new ISO standards, of new OECD or IMF guidance, of new indicators, rankings, and benchmarking—it is to experience a peculiar pleasure at having more rules and control mechanisms to submit to or to implement (or both)—books such as *The Joy of SOX: Why Sarbanes–Oxley and Service-Oriented Architecture May Be the Best Thing That Ever Happened to You* (Taylor, 2006) only testify to the libidinal economy of compliance, the joys of submission and the joys of enforcement. But, as we shall see, there are also the joys of corporate sovereignty, of breaking the law in the name of the law.

Compliance is still largely a foreign concept to the many ordinary citizens, despite its march to the foreground during the COVID-19 pandemic (Rollason & Hirsch, 2021); even in the academic circles of criminologists and anthropologists, the compliance industry often needs an introduction. And yet, both the concept and the industry are transforming public and private organizations, corporations, and workplaces from within, enlisting these in the fight against crime, harm, and moral failings both directed at outsiders and their own, and in the process submitting all to risk assessments that assign colours and scores to their likelihood of being a criminal, a threat, or a security or reputational risk. While there are ongoing discussions about whether compliance is mere 'paper compliance', a corporate façade to improve and manufacture corporate reputations, a mere 'window dressing', or 'box ticking', or a genuine effort to do the right thing, an effort to embed ethical cultures and induce social change (Sampson, 2021), these discussions I argue serve as a mere *distraction* from the more fundamental transfers of power to which we are witness. While this form of critique do indeed have a point that compliance quickly becomes an exercise in paper production, that it is inefficient, a mere exercise in ethics washing and so on (Péretz & Picard, 2015; van Rooij & Fine, 2020), what is demanded in the aftermath of this critique is typically *more* of the same in addition to (this time) 'real' transformation towards ethical culture. We can thus read that,

> despite the science, the law continues to favor compliance management, whistleblower protection, and monitoring arrangements as "best practices" to reduce corporate misconduct. The law is not alone here in supporting these unproven internal approaches to deal with corporate wrongdoing. For businesses, internal compliance management, whistleblower protection, and monitoring, while costly, are strategies to alleviate legal sanctions or reduce liability. In many cases, these strategies even provide an opportunity to restore their reputation – sometimes (and ideally), like Siemens, going from fraud villain to compliance hero. Meanwhile, the people whose job it is to regulate or prosecute corporate misconduct often fail to publicly express strong concerns about the effectiveness of these internal systems. Prosecutors and regulators appear continually pressed to show that they take corporate wrongdoing seriously, while being structurally challenged to create actual deterrence. The best they can hope for after a major scandal is the proud press release of another multibillion-dollar settlement, with the installation of compliance management and monitoring to signal their commitment to future risk prevention, and maybe – if they get lucky – a successful verdict against individual executives. For most regulators, and especially prosecutors, achieving sustained behavioral change is simply not their most pressing concern. (van Rooij & Fine, 2020, p. 240)

This essay is concerned with what this *more* actually does, whom and what does this compliance architecture serve—if not the prosecution of corporate crime? It may be inefficient in its stated purpose, but it appears, in a manner of a 'function creep' (Koops, 2021), far more efficient in other ways, ways that have so far evaded direct critique. Verhage rightly recognized that the compliance industry is best analysed within the framework of privatization and pluralization of *policing* (Verhage, 2011). And it is from this vantage point that we shall analyse the compliance-industrial complex. Whether compliance is faked or genuine, efficient in its stated missions or not, what matters for us that compliance is *de facto* a policing and governance function legitimized by recourse to ethics, created on demand from and mandated by the state. What we are dealing with here is not mere contractualization or outsourcing, but a privatization and pluralization of policing and the securitization of ethics at a more fundamental level. To understand this, we must transgress the otherwise enlightening discussions on outsourcing of state functions and concrete tasks to private prisons, private military contractors, and private security companies (Fitzgibbon & Lea, 2020). There are deeper forms of delegation of state authority, sovereignty, and power—hiding in plain sight. Even though instrumental in the transformation of governance, consent manufacturing, control, and policing, they often evade the compartmentalized and hyper-specialized disciplinary gaze. Compliance—in a sense of both an industry and a transversal set of governance practices—speaks to a particular regulatory and governance logic that is gaining traction in national, supranational, and global context. Governance *through* compliance, and its particular modalities as they will be outlined here, is already shaping the ways in which we are ruled, controlled, coerced, and subjected. I argue that what we see emerging is *criminalized and securitized data-driven and intelligence-led compliance as a new hybrid mode of governance that crosses geographical as well as imaginary boundaries between the public and the private, that is legitimized by the global fight against corruption and transnational organized crime and that enhances corporate sovereignty rather than setting limits to it.* The expansion of this compliance logic demands critical criminological and anthropological engagement. This transformation of compliance into *governance* gives the *compliance-industrial complex* disproportionate power over our lives. Despite this, the compliance-industrial complex has so far not been properly recognized as an industrial complex in its own right. Compliance is, I argue, a part of the 'global industrial complex'—of the 'tangled matrix of systems anchored in logics of control, standardization, exploitation, and profit', a part of the expansive, colonizing, interconnected network (…) comprised of numerous industry-capital specific systems such as the criminal industrial complex, the agricultural industrial complex, the medical industrial complex, the animal industrial complex, the academic industrial complex, the military industrial complex, the prison industrial complex, the entertainment industrial complex, and the communication industrial complex (…) dominated by capitalist growth and profit imperatives, bureaucratic efficiency requirements, technological mass production standardization, and hierarchical administration, and is backed by punishment, jail, and military force. (Best, 2011, pp. xix–xxii)

At the same time, compliance is, paradoxically, enhancing rather than undermining 'corporate sovereignty' (Barkan, 2013; Diphoorn & Wiegnick, 2021). Corporate sovereignty is best understood as 'based on the use of both the punitive understandings of sovereign power and the "soft" forms of power linked to agendas of human progress' (Diphoorn & Wiegnick, 2021, p. 426). Our case shows how the state actively manufactures corporate sovereignty, giving corporations special privileges, or the 'sovereign gift' (Barkan, 2013, p. 19). In our case, this 'sovereign gift' naturally follows from anti-policies that demand both legal and moral compliance in the name of combatting security threats, it is through these policies that the state effectively delegates parts of its sovereign power to corporations. Indeed,

Hobbes's anxiety, and his peculiar resolution of it in the form of the sovereign gift, continues to trouble the world. The power granted to corporations enabled them to discipline both members and nonmembers, promoting a host of activities that benefited the sovereign. By disciplining individuals in poorhouses, orphanages, towns, religious orders, and hospitals, corporations used their legally granted privileges to produce forms of life that were proper or valuable for the state. (Barkan, 2013, p. 38)

Compliance, mandated by different anti-policies, reproduces the same logic. Alas, this often goes unnoticed. Corporations tend to complain of 'regulatory burdens', of the 'costs of compliance', and of the ever-proliferating regulations to which they need to 'submit' and comply with. But this talk of compliance costs effectively hides the transfer of power, authority, and sovereignty, one that can be easily repurposed for managerial control and policing. While having some risk management, internal control mechanisms, and accountability systems in place may indeed be reasonable and necessary in order to pursue legitimate business interests, our concern here is with this particular logic of governance becoming *excessive*. When excessive, it can quickly flip into its opposite, into unreason, and into a destructive force; its hollow and reductionist nature and its tendency towards individual responsibilization further enhance corporate power.

The aim of this essay is to make us think more critically about the inherent logic and possible effects of overreliance on hyper-securitized and criminalized compliance as a mode of governance. The word 'compliance' and the compliance industry may seem foreign and unfamiliar or the sound of them even boring and tedious to many, but this may be even more reason to burst the benign bubble of appearances. Indeed, technobureaucracy may be both tedious and boring, but its power is not to be underestimated and neither the old proverb that the road to hell is paved with good intentions; we should, also, not dismiss the possibility that there may be lurking the 'banality of evil' (Arendt, 1965) and administrative violence if compliance gets to unfold into its extremes and loses sight of the unintended consequences of its everyday and routine technical acts. This essay is therefore also speculative and cautionary, trying to capture the direction in which the governance and control of the social are moving and what its costs may turn out to be. It tries to make us think about the ways we seek to control the globalized world and the evils in it, and the ways in which we end up being controlled in the process. A world where demands for *more* technobureaucratic control in the name of security and anti-crime policies proliferate, despite their failures. At the same time, the repeated failures, which paradoxically stimulate the drive for more of the same (and more failure), may be blinding us to alternative ways of imagining and tackling the same challenges. It may also be that we are not only choosing the wrong methods, but also creating pseudo-solutions that prevent us from actually addressing the very real crimes, risks, security threats, and harms and that divert our attention away from the transfer of state power to corporations, while generating new and often unrecognized 'administrative crimes', harms, and injustices. We can all agree that efforts to tackle financial and white-collar crime should be intensified, but the question is whether the ways we keep going about this intensification not only paradoxically prevent us from making serious progress but also generate new harms, which reproduce and exaggerate rather than undermine existing inequalities.

References

Arendt, H. (1965). *Eichmann in Jerusalem: A report on the banality of evil.* Viking Press.

Arlen, J., & Buell, S. W. (2020). The law of corporate investigations and the global expansion of corporate criminal enforcement. *Southern California Law Review, 93,* 697–761.

Bacchi, C. (2000). Policy as discourse: What does it mean? Where does it get us? *Discourse: Studies in the Cultural Politics of Education, 21*(1), 45–57. https://doi.org/10.1080/01596300050005493

Barkan, J. (2013). *Corporate sovereignty: Law and government under capitalism.* University of Minnesota Press. https://doi.org/10.5749/minnesota/9780816674268.001.0001

Ben Jaffel, H., & Larsson, S. (2022). Introduction: What's the problem with intelligence studies? Outlining a new research agenda on contemporary intelligence. In H. Ben Jaffel & S. Larsson (Eds.), *Problematising intelligence studies: Towards a new research agenda* (pp. 3–29). Routledge. https://doi.org/10.4324/9781003205463-2

Best, S. (2011). Pathologies of power and the rise of the global industrial complex. In S. Best, R. Kahn, A. J. Nocella, & P. McLaren (Eds.), *The global industrial complex: Systems of domination* (pp. ix–xxv). Lexington Books.

Braithwaite, J. (2008). *Regulatory capitalism: How it works, ideas for making it better.* Edward Elgar. https://doi.org/10.4337/9781848441262

Buzan, B., Wæver, O., & de Wilde, J. (1998). *Security: A new framework for analysis.* Lynne Rienner. https://doi.org/10.1515/9781685853808

Cohn, C. (1987). Sex and death in the rational world of defense intellectuals. *Signs, 12*(4), 687–718. https://doi.org/10.1086/494362

Diphoorn, T., & Wiegnick, N. (2021, September). Corporate sovereignty: Negotiating permissive power for profit in Southern Africa. *Anthropological Theory, 22*(4), 422–442. https://doi.org/10.1177/14634996211037124

Easterling, K. (2016). *Extrastatecraft: The power of infrastructure space.* Verso.

Fisher, M. (2009). *Capitalist realism: Is there no alternative?* Zero Books.

Fitzgibbon, W., & Lea, J. (2020). *Privatising justice: The security industry.* Pluto Press. https://doi.org/10.2307/j.ctvzsmdsj

Frischmann, B., & Selinger, E. (2018). *Re-engineering humanity.* Cambridge University Press. https://doi.org/10.1017/9781316544846

Glasbeek, H. (2018). *Capitalism: A crime story.* Between The Lines.

Grabosky, P. (2013). Beyond responsive regulation: The expanding role of non-state actors in the regulatory process. *Regulation & Governance, 7,* 114–123. https://doi.org/10.1111/j.1748-5991.2012.01147.x

Koops, B.-J. (2021). The concept of function creep. *Law, Innovation and Technology, 13*(1), 29–56. https://doi.org/10.1080/17579961.2021.1898299

Kuldova, T. Ø., & Nordrik, B. (forthcoming). Workplace investigations and the hollowing out of the Norwegian model of co-determination. *Class and Capital.*

Levi-Faur, D. (2005). The global diffusion of regulatory capitalism. *The Annals of the American Academy of Political and Social Science, 598*, 12–32. https://doi.org/10.1177/0002716204272371

Levi-Faur, D. (2017). Regulatory capitalism. In P. Drahos (Ed.), *Regulatory theory: Foundation and applications* (pp. 289–302). ANU Press. https://doi.org/10.22459/RT.02.2017.17

McGoey, L. (2012). Philanthrocapitalism and its critics. *Poetics, 40*, 185–199. https://doi.org/10.1016/j.poetic.2012.02.006

Mills, C. W. (2000). *Sociological imagination.* Oxford University Press.

Nordrik, B., & Kuldova, T. Ø. (2021). *Faktaundersøkelser - et "hybrid konflikt-tvåpen" på norske arbeidsplasser.* Gyldendal Akademisk.

Nyquist, A., & Leivestad, H. (Eds.). (2017). *Ethnographies of conferences and trade fairs: Shaping industries.* Palgrave Macmillan.

Østbø, J. (2017). Securitizing "spiritual-moral values" in Russia. *Post-Soviet Affairs, 33*(3), 200–216. https://doi.org/10.1080/1060586X.2016.1251023

Péretz, M., & Picard, S. (2015). Compliance or comfort zone? The work of embedded ethics in performing regulation. *Journal of Business Ethics, 131*(4), 833–852. https://doi.org/10.1007/s10551-014-2154-3

Petersen, K. L., & Tjalve, V. S. (2013). (Neo) Republican security governance? US homeland security and the politics of "shared responsibility". *International Political Sociology, 7*(1), 1–18. https://doi.org/10.1111/ips.12006

Power, M. (1997). *The audit society: Rituals of verification.* Oxford University Press.

Ragazzi, F. (2017). Countering terrorism and radicalisation: Securitising social policy? *Critical Social Policy, 37*(2), 163–179. https://doi.org/10.1177/0261018316683472

Rollason, W., & Hirsch, E. (2021). Compliance: Politics, sociability and the constitution of collective life. *Journal of Legal Anthropology, 5*(1), 1–31. https://doi.org/10.3167/jla.2021.050101

Sampson, S. (2021). Good people doing bad things: Compliance regimes in organisations. *Journal of Legal Anthropology, 5*(1), 110–134. https://doi.org/10.3167/jla.2021.050105

Sataøen, H. L. (2018). Regulokratene: Den nye styringsprofesjonen? *Norsk sosiologisk tidsskrift, 2*(6), 481–499. https://doi.org/10.18261/issn.2535-2512-2018-06-03

Schuilenburg, M. (2011). The securitization of society: On the rise of quasi-criminal law and selective exclusion. *Social Justice, 38*(1/2), 73–89.

Shore, C., & Wright, S. (2015). Audit culture revisited: Rankings, ratings, and the reassembling of society. *Current Anthropology, 56*(3), 421–444. https://doi.org/10.1086/681534

Supiot, A. (2017). *Governance by numbers: The making of a legal model of allegiance.* Bloomsbury.

Taylor, H. (2006). *The joy of SOX: Why Sarbanes-Oxley and service-oriented architecture may be the best thing that ever happened to you.* Wiley.

Underkuffler, L. S. (2013). *Captured by evil: The idea of corruption in law.* Yale University Press.

van Rooij, B., & Fine, A. D. (2020). Preventing corporate crime from within: Compliance management, whistleblowing and internal monitoring. In M. L. Rorie (Ed.), *The handbook of white-collar crime.* Wiley. https://doi.org/10.1002/9781118775004.ch15

Veggeland, N. (2009). *Taming the regulatory state: Politics and ethics.* Edward Elgar. https://doi.org/10.4337/9781848447509

Verhage, A. (2011). *The anti money laundering complex and the compliance industry.* Routledge. https://doi.org/10.4324/9780203828489

Willis, P. (2000). *The ethnographic imagination.* Polity Press.

Woodiwiss, M. (2005). *Gangster capitalism: The United States and the global rise of organized crime.* Constable.

Žižek, S. (2009). *First as tragedy, then as farce.* Verso. http://books.google.com/books?id=HRX4DSJuGtUC

Zuboff, S. (2019). *The age of surveillance capitalism: The fight for a human future at the new frontier of power.* Profile Books.

CHAPTER 2

The Anti-policy Syndrome

Abstract We proceed to consider the 'anti-policy syndrome', the understanding of which is key for our consequent discussion of the compliance-
industrial complex. We return to the *United States Strategy on Countering
Corruption* introduced in Chapter 1 and dig deeper into the logic of
consensus-driven anti-policies aimed at tackling crimes and evils alike.
We examine more closely how anti-policies become integrated into each
other, look at regulatory hybridization and blurring, and at how these
processes are prefiguring the integration of anti-policies into the logic of
compliance while also prefiguring the platformization of compliance. We
take on the endless expansion of the risk universe, the manufacturing of
risks and threats, and the simultaneous fetishization of technosolutionism
and compliance as *the* answer to very different crimes and risks.

Keywords Anti-policy syndrome · Technosolutionism · Risk ·
Compliance · Regulatory hybridization

The growth of the compliance-industrial complex as we shall see owes
to the growth of regulation, and more specifically, to the growth of
anti-policies. Let us therefore return to our paradigmatic example, the
United States Strategy on Countering Corruption. Strategies such as this
one tell us what issues and problems need fixing, how they are to be

understood, and how they are best to be tackled. Policy documents and declarations that seek to combat or counter one evil or another are popular. For good reason, all can agree upon them, or at least, upon their importance. They are capable of generating multilateral agreement and collective actions: the 'fights against…' and the 'wars on…'—corruption, terrorism financing, drugs, human rights abuses, human trafficking, transnational organized crime, sexual harassment, environmental destruction, and so on. Anti-policies build *consensus* around that which nobody can be for (Walters, 2008). They are typically fuelled by scandals and mediated outrage. As such, they are a seductive tool. After all, to be seen doing 'the right thing' is a vital currency in a world driven by reputations and scandals. And with each scandal we also see this demand for remedy: more anti-policies, more zero tolerance visions (Newburn & Jones, 2007), more ethical guidelines, more standards and best practices, more accountability, more audits, and more detailed implementations of the principles of 'good governance', all of which seek to eradicate this or that crime, harm, or moral failing (Shore, 2008; Shore & Wright, 2015). The evil cannot be tolerated; we must show that we are on the side of the good. Across the globe, corporations proudly declare their zero tolerance anti-policies, be it Siemens,[1] ING,[2] or Petrobras[3] and so do political leaders, from the Prime Minister Narendra Modi of India[4] via the First Lady Janet Kataaha Museveni of Uganda[5] to Prime Minister Sheikh Hasina of Bangladesh,[6] they all repeat the same: good governance, accountability, integrity, ethics, transparency, and of course, zero tolerance for any *deviation* from ethics and set procedures. But what is actually being implemented in the name of these values and visions?

[1] https://new.siemens.com/us/en/company/about/compliance.html (last accessed August 2, 2022).

[2] https://www.ing.com/About-us/Compliance/Zero-Tolerance-Bribery-Statement.htm (last accessed August 2, 2022).

[3] https://petrobras.com.br/en/about-us/profile/compliance-ethics-and-transparency/ (last accessed August 2, 2022).

[4] https://www.hindustantimes.com/india-news/atcbicvcmeet-pm-calls-for-zero-tolerance-to-corruption-101634754349769.html (last accessed August 2, 2022).

[5] https://allafrica.com/stories/202110210123.html (last accessed August 2, 2022).

[6] https://www.thedailystar.net/opinion/news/governments-zero-tolerance-policy-against-corruption-1702171 (last accessed August 2, 2022).

Consensus-driven anti-policies often tend to close down possibilities for critical and principled political debate. After all, 'something' needs to be done and every step in the 'right direction' is easily appreciated and touted as progress. But we should always ask—in what directions are we being pushed in the name of the good? How are these anti-policies framing the issue and mobilizing our affects (Lordon, 2014)? Are they setting limits to what can be said, thought and what actions are deemed legitimate and designated as 'best practice' (and by whom)? What are we *for* when we are against corruption and all the other range of evils (as defined and as combatted by these anti-policies and their regulatory twins)?

On the Expanding Risk Universe

The *United States Strategy on Countering Corruption* tells us that this fight against corruption is to target corruption in its many and multiplying forms: from bribery, administrative corruption, grand corruption, kleptocracy, state capture, to strategic corruption—the evolving threat of the weaponization of corrupt practices as a tenet of foreign policy. Corruption thus comes in many forms, in different scales and so do corruption risks. In other words, we are witness to strategic expansion and policy stretching of the concept of 'corruption' to encompass ever new signifieds (Kajsiu, 2021). This increases the scope of problems and harms that are to be targeted through anti-corruption. This aligns also with the emphasis of the anti-corruption strategy on the fact that the fight *against* corruption can no longer be seen as separate from all the other battles against related forms of evils and other undesirable states of both domestic and global affairs. Different governmental agencies and departments thus need to cooperate with each other and across jurisdictions, and most importantly, join forces with the private sector which devises the solutions for compliance with all these new anti-policies and regulations.

This strategic stretching is easily discernible across policy papers that regularly open by stating the difficulty of pinpointing what corruption is, citing the simplistic definition of corruption as bribery and abuse of entrusted power or public office for private gain, only to reject it as not comprehensive enough, finally claiming that there is no universal definition. Instead, the reader is bombarded with concrete examples of an extreme multitude of transnational phenomena, crimes, and social harms: bribery, embezzlement, fraud, theft, collusion, clientelism, favouritism, nepotism, conflict of interest, and more. These are then quickly linked to money laundering, tax evasion, illicit capital flight, illegal trafficking of drugs, arms and humans, human rights abuses, environmental crimes, and more. Together, they are then linked to various *impacts* and *threats*, from threats to democracy and development to national security, which are further linked to *estimates* of financial losses, some of the most popular being the estimate of costs of corruption to be 5% of world's GDP, which has circulated in UN, World Bank, and related circles for about a decade, and was mentioned for instance in a speech by Kamala Harris in May 2021,[7] and *perceptions* of prevalence of corruption, such as the Corruption Perception Index by Transparency International. PwC has recently estimated that USD 1 trillion is paid in bribes globally each year, while USD 2.6 trillion are lost to corruption, designating it the 'single biggest issue facing today's society'.[8] As with other popular estimates and quantifications, these often turn out to lack credibility and are unfounded and deeply problematic. A recent critical review of corruption statistics featuring prominently in policy papers, speeches, and multiple documents across the anti-corruption industry concluded as follows: 'The results of our investigation are disheartening. Of the ten corruption statistics we assessed, not a single one could be classified as credible' (Wathne & Stephenson, 2021, p. 2). These results can appear shocking, but are actually widely known, or at least suspected, and disavowed; the problem is not a lack of knowledge but rather the opposite, its 'strategic ignorance' (McGoey, 2019). The same logic manifests in the US anti-corruption strategy, which starts by listing the various dramatic *impacts* of corruption, offering few *examples*, and stating that 'corruption takes on many forms and is used to further various illicit behaviors' (p. 6), only to quote an exemplary number: 'for example, every year an estimated $88.6 billion—equivalent to 3.7 percent of Africa's GDP—leaves the continent in the form of illicit capital flight' (p. 6). Such examples, impacts, estimates, and threats that feature prominently across policy papers are best viewed as rhetorical devices, which, chanted like mantras, repeatedly, in different iterations, give the global fight against corruption and the anti-corruption measures their legitimatory and moral force. This is in no way

---

[7] https://www.politifact.com/factchecks/2021/may/07/kamala-harris/kamala-harris-said-corruption-costs-much-5-worlds-/ (last accessed February 2, 2022).

[8] https://www.pwc.com/gx/en/forensics/five-forces-that-will-reshape-the-landscape-of-anti-bribery-and-anti-corruption-final.pdf (last accessed April 21, 2022).

to deny the magnitude of social harms resulting from all these exemplary crimes and other 'lawful but awful' practices, but to say that they are strategically repeated, cited, and invoked in a ritualistic manner both to establish one's moral superiority and to legitimize the actual punitive measures, regulations, and sanctions regimes that are implemented to tackle corruption. Corruption has over time moved away from being conceived in narrow economic and narrow moral terms, predominantly linked to matters of developmental economic policies, often designed to spread neoliberal reforms across the globe (Katzarova, 2019), to encompass ever greater swathes of real and moral phenomena. From the initial debates about the morality of the markets and the '*moral underpinnings* of a successful market' (Bukovansky, 2006, p. 182; emphasis in original), the language of anti-corruption has been progressively more moralistic or moralizing and more encompassing, while simultaneously managing 'to evade and obscure, rather than directly engage, core problems of politics and ethics' (Bukovansky, 2006, p. 182). The confusion about what corruption is and the strategic ignorance and evasion of the core problems of politics and ethics is matched only by the confidence about how to fight and prevent corruption. The solutions, too, may go under different names, but they are all framed in the universalizing terms of 'good governance' and 'best practice' (Mungiu-Pippidi, 2021), accompanied by key concepts such as 'integrity', 'transparency', 'accountability', and 'risk management'. Concepts that become, upon closer look, strikingly hollow.

Corruption can in other words no longer be thought as separate: it is weaved into a global threat, security, and risk landscape—into a whole range of other risks big and small, million-dollar fraud schemes and unethical behaviours alike. Or else, it is weaved into the 'compliance and risk universe' as the compliance industry likes to call it. Ernst and Young thus ask in a blog post: 'How Can Finite Resources Tackle Infinite Risk Universe?',[9] OECD explains in its report 'Analytics for Integrity: Data-Driven Approaches For Enhancing Corruption And Fraud Risk Assessments' how the use of data analytics can 'help managers to understand the risk universe and take preventive actions in response' (OECD, 2019, p. 27), while Cosmos, the new online platform from the Society of Corporate Compliance and Ethics & Health Care Compliance Association, promises to help us 'navigate the compliance

---

[9] https://www.ey.com/en_gl/risk/how-can-finite-resources-tackle-an-infinite-risk-uni verse (last accessed August 9, 2022).

universe'.[10] And we could go on. An expanding universe is the metaphor the compliance-industrial complex lives by (Lakoff & Johnson, 2003).

Risks and threats appear to lurk everywhere, under ever new guises and in ever new shades. Manufactured or real? It becomes difficult to tell nor does it matter. Whether manufactured or real, they become real in their consequences, to apply the Thomas theorem. While in the fast-expanding real universe dark and mysterious forces are pulling galaxies apart, in the fast-expanding compliance universe, galaxies of risks, security threats, and crime scenarios are being pulled *together* by regulatory and capital forces. While these may appear as dark and mysterious, they appear as such since fetishized; risk transforms in a fantasy that acts as a structuring illusion, an illusion that structures reality and social activity (Kuldova, 2019; Žižek, 1989). This is in no way to say that all risks are illusory, but to say that they become an *ideological fantasy*, one that structures the 'compliance universe', its material and ritual practices, and its understanding of the world; a fantasy that interpellates us as subjects (Althusser, 1971). The ideological fantasy of the expansive risk universe serves not only capital accumulation, mirroring the fantasy of eternal and unlimited growth, but also our subjectivation as (morally) risky subjects and subjects at (moral) risk. As such, it can be deemed a 'dominant fiction', a category of hegemony consisting of the 'images and stories through which a society figures consensus' (Silverman, 2016, p. 30); consensus-driven anti-policies are its concrete expression. It is not a coincidence that the US anti-corruption strategy prioritizes the 'development of a common understanding of corruption risks':

> The U.S. Government will prioritize the development of a common understanding of corruption risks through joint analyses that outline corruption dynamics, networks, and nodes; consider enablers and drivers of corrupt behavior; examine the potential impact of providing foreign assistance (including security sector assistance); and identify possible entry points or levers to shift the dynamics of corruption in order to incentivize reform. This common understanding will serve as a basis for consultations between Washington, U.S. embassies overseas, and the interagency to inform decision-makers as they weigh trade-offs associated with U.S. assistance and mitigate risks. As part of this work, foreign assistance agencies will strive to better "know their partner" and map the vectors of corruption

---

[10] https://compliancecosmos.org/ (last accessed August 9, 2022).

in the benefiting country, including through consultation with intelligence, law enforcement, journalists, and civil society organizations.

Risk analysis is also positioned as a way to 'know' one's partner, way to know the Other. The same logic manifests in due diligence, such as in KYC (know your customer) or EDD (enhanced due diligence), now being transformed into KYD (know your data), where the Other is authenticated, verified, and consequently reduced to a composite risk score based on the assessment of a range of proxies, indicators of risk, and patterns of financial and social transactions. Increasingly, we seek to 'know' and govern the Other through risk, through precaution. As Aradau and van Munster argue, this 'precautionary principle privileges a politics of speed based on the sovereign decision on dangerousness' (Aradau & van Munster, 2007, p. 107), a sovereign decision that is delegated, along with its management to the compliance-industrial complex, among others.

The expansion of the risk universe and the proliferation of anti-policies are mutually constitutive, stimulating the growth of the compliance-industrial complex. The insistence of anti-policies to see risks, threats, and crime scenarios as integrated is further transformed into 'holistic' and 'integrated' approaches and solutions to risk management: anything from anti-corruption and anti-money laundering to sexual harassment and problematic utterances can be tackled from the same platform, using the same logic. All one needs is to implement 'good governance' and internal control procedures, fine-tune risk assessments, install suspicious activity monitoring and detection systems, or even predictive surveillance technologies. The multiplication of guidelines and rules, codes of conduct, standards, committees, and so on, accompanied by reporting, accounting, monitoring, bureaucratic procedures, risk assessments, investigations, and surveillance, stimulates the growth and creates demand for 'professionals in the management of unease' (Bigo, 2002, p. 64) and for supporting technobureaucratic 'bullshit jobs' (Graeber, 2018). Upon closer inspection, many of these forms, rules, codes, regulations, and professions appear conspicuously empty, but even here, in the risk 'universe', we should concur with Albert Einstein who realized that 'empty space is not nothing'.[11]

[11] https://science.nasa.gov/astrophysics/focus-areas/what-is-dark-energy (last accessed August 9, 2022).

ON STANDING (MORALLY) UNITED
AGAINST ... A THREAT TO OUR SECURITY

Anti-corruption stands out among the anti-policies; it is not only paradigmatic but also serves as *the* umbrella narrative: corruption as a concept and imaginary is capable of mobilizing popular passions and affects and thus of fuelling the righteous fight against all that is bad, criminal, suspicious, and undesirable. Merely labelling something corrupt, or linking it to corruption, can easily legitimize and mobilize support for agendas that could be potentially far more politically controversial—for instance the 'war on cash' (in the interest of FinTechs and other financial institutions) waged in the name of 'financial inclusion' and the fight against corruption, terrorism financing, and money laundering (Scott, 2022). Corruption as a concept serves as a *proxy* for ruin, decay, disorder, and dirt—a moral concept that can be stretched and encompass far more than the limited legal definitions of 'bribery' or 'trading in influence'. Corruption is framed as a moral failing with the most destructive consequences—or as Pope Francis put it, corruption is 'evil' and 'offends human dignity'.[12] To reiterate, the fight against corruption has been transformed from one defined largely in economic and developmental terms which were *legitimized* through recourse to *particular* notions of morality of the markets fostering 'virtuous behavior' (Wolf, 2003, pp. 47–48), to one defined in *moral* terms and thus stretching beyond the sphere of economy into the securitization of this morality (Østbø, 2017) and 'criminalization of compliance' (Haugh, 2017). Precisely due to its moral force and hence its ability to legitimize regulations and policies, corruption forms the ideological core of the compliance-industrial complex. We are thus not merely dealing with the demands on regulatory compliance here, but with strategies that allow for values and ethics, or rather for 'simulacra of morality' (MacIntyre, 2007, p. 2), to be securitized, consequently legitimizing managerial practices (in the name of the good) that would otherwise be far more contentious. And since we are dealing with 'simulacra of morality', there never seems to be *enough* effort put into ensuring ethical compliance; there is never enough compliance.

The global fight against corruption and financial crime has in other words provided something that global governance actors could easily

---

[12] https://twitter.com/Pontifex/status/939472199878103041 (last accessed June 1, 2022).

unite around: after all, nobody can be *for* corruption, *for* financial crime, or *for* terrorism financing. The fight against corruption and calls for transparency and 'good governance' gained momentum in the mid-1990s. In 1996, John Wolfensohn, then president of the World Bank, delivered his infamous speech on the 'cancer of corruption', in 1997, UN General Secretary Kofi Annan deemed corruption 'evil and insidious', and the OECD signed the Anti-Bribery Convention (1997) followed by the United Nation's Convention Against Corruption (2003). Biden's strategy is just one of the latest iterations of this expanding and increasingly integrated regime of global crime and security governance, which sits alongside proliferating maze of EU anti-corruption and AML regulation, directives, legislation, and bodies such as GRECO, OLAF, FATF, and so on, far too many to even list,[13] and along the UN's Sustainable Development Goals (16.5. and 16.6.) and UN Global Compact, each of these with their indicators and measures of the 'good'. The fight against corruption, as Biden's strategy lays out, is now a matter of national security which also means that it is to be even more tightly integrated into anti-money laundering (AML), countering the financing of terrorism (CFT), sanctions, the use of the Sanctions Act to counter America's Adversaries,[14] tax rules enforcement, and related systems. As the strategy declares, 'corrupt actors exploit deficiencies' in these systems and 'corrupt elites and non-state armed groups enrich themselves through illicit proceeds and trade of high-value commodities' while exploiting 'rule-of-law-based societies' who 'continue to provide entry points for corrupt actors to launder their funds and their reputations'.[15] When it comes to anti-corruption and related regulation, governments have chosen to depend on obtaining compliance of actors within the private sector, on monitoring this compliance, issuing guidance on compliance programs, on deterrents, threats of punishment, fines and sanctions of violators and those with deficient compliance programs, and on the ability to influence other jurisdictions and dissuade actors within the evasion industry, such as sanctions busters, facilitators of offshore havens, and other 'unaccountables' (Wedel, 2014). In line with this, the strategy thus targets both

---

[13] https://ec.europa.eu/home-affairs/corruptionen (last accessed April 21, 2022).

[14] https://home.treasury.gov/system/files/126/caatsaeo.pdf (last accessed February, 27, 2022).

[15] https://www.whitehouse.gov/wp-content/uploads/2021/12/United-States-Strategy-on-Countering-Corruption.pdf (last accessed January 31, 2022), p. 7.

domestic and foreign actors, while enlisting a broad coalition of partners, public, private, multilateral, NGOs, and more into the anti-corruption fight, where corruption is both cause and symptom of a broad range of other crimes and harms. This fight will thus not only require a 'whole-of-government' approach, beyond the Department of Justice (DOJ), thus involving more actively the intelligence community and other key departments, but also increased collaboration with the private sector and the strengthening and expansion of compliance programs. While the strategy aims to improve existing tools, increase law enforcement resources and information sharing, expand investigative tools, launch new legislation expanding criminal law, enhance beneficial ownership disclosures and sanctions regimes, strengthen the international multilateral architecture, and more, it sends a strong message to the private sector.

Elevating corruption to a matter of national security and increasing funding dedicated to combatting it—no longer as a 'mere' criminal offence, signals increased risks for companies with insufficient compliance systems and an expectation on the private sector to further strengthen AML, CFT, due diligence, and anti-corruption compliance. The anti-corruption strategy, elevating corruption as a moral evil into the realm of national security threats, such as terrorism, thus enables these fights to merge even more smoothly, to become integrated not only in terms of strategic co-operation, but also in terms of their inner logic. We can draw a parallel here between the legal obligations to implement compliance programs in regulated entities, underpinned by moral obligations to fight financial crime, to the logic of UK's Prevent Duty. The latter has been implemented under the Counter-Terrorism and Security Act of 2015, which 'puts a legal duty on specified authorities such as health, education, probation, and local government, to prevent people from "being drawn into terrorism" (…) as such, the policy turns teachers, lecturers, doctors, and social workers into agents of states, their interactions with the public become acts of surveillance, and the spaces they occupy turn into sites of pre-emptive policing' (Kaleem, 2022, p. 73). The same can be said of the compliance officers, of the HR managers, IT developers, and engineers that increasingly see themselves as pre-empting crime, fraud, misconduct, harassment, and so on. As Kaleem points out, Prevent Strategy, and we could again argue the same for AML, anti-corruption, CFT, and so on,

> established a new way of doing intelligence by co-opting everyday practices and sites of activities, and in the process have made intelligence gathering a

normal activity for citizens tasked with these responsibilities (…) the intelligence regime established by Prevent is novel as it is both obligatory and appeals to citizens voluntary tendencies. It legitimises suspicion-making but justifies it as an act of safeguarding. (Kaleem, 2022, p. 74)

The same dynamics encompasses also our 'professional managers of unease' (Bigo, 2002) in compliance, who direct their gaze at employees, clients, suppliers, and others they deal with and legitimize their suspicion-making by recourse to the moral imperatives of fighting transnational crimes and security threats. But whereas Prevent appeals more directly to civic duty and duty of care, corporate compliance invokes this civic duty, especially on the side of the compliance officer, but it integrates it further into the visions of corporate citizenship, ethical business, CSR, and stakeholder capitalism. In both Prevent and other anti-policies, we can therefore discern a 'two-pronged approach of an obligatory framework operationalised through consensual politics' that co-opts 'practices, actors and sites within a new intelligence regime', making 'civilian-led intelligence gathering a ubiquitous activity' (Kaleem, 2022, p. 89). While anti-policies utilizing public sector have received more attention as the enlisting of teachers or health care and social workers in counter-radicalization immediately triggers concerns about the latter being incompatible with their professions, we see here that the same intelligence-led and pre-emptive policing is demanded from the private sector employees; they become the agents *through* which the state is to fight crimes and harms. In the latter case, however, this move increases corporate power and corporate sovereignty, while legitimizing intrusive managerial practices, as we shall see later on.

ON TECHNOSOLUTIONISM

The US anti-corruption strategy furthermore makes clear that 'encouraging the adoption and enforcement of anti-corruption compliance programs by U.S. and international companies' (p. 12) is to be linked to the utilization of new technological tools and innovation in the fight against corruption (Objective 5.3). The strategy emphasizes the importance of increased support to state and non-state partners, investigative journalists, whistleblowers, activists, and the promotion of 'public-private partnerships to more consistently bring in the private sector as critical actors in the fight against corruption' (p. 8). In other words, one of the key strategic aims is the further *expansion* of the compliance-industrial complex, and in particular, the implementation of new data-driven RegTech solutions to the increasingly intertwined AML, anti-corruption, CFT, sanctions, and related regulatory compliance as well as further increased involvement of a wide range of private actors and public–private partnerships in crime prevention, in the governance of transnational crime, and in 'global norm institutionalization' (Jakobi, 2017). The strategy thus affords increased power and legitimacy to the compliance industry and RegTech as industries key not only to policing and preventing corruption and transnational organized crime, but also to governance (Hansen & Tang-Jensen, 2015).

The *United States Strategy on Countering Corruption* can thus be said to align smoothly with the interests of this expansive industry in stimulating the growth of the regulatory as well as voluntary self-regulatory architectures which naturally translate into new markets for compliance, audit, and intelligence—a prominent feature of 'regulatory capitalism' (Levi-Faur, 2017). But it also aligns well with the RegTech industry's hunger for data and data analytics monetization and exploitation of the possibilities that lie in OSINT and other trends well captured by the concept of 'surveillance capitalism' (Zuboff, 2019), where data-mining technologies are best understood as not in any way neutral, but as technologies of governance and power, shaped by concrete interests (Campbell-Verduyn et al., 2017; Johns, 2017; Kalpokas, 2019; Katzenbach & Ulbricht, 2019). While this insertion of 'corporate crime fighters' and non-state actors into global crime and security governance and regulatory processes, as well as the role of states and public authorities in privatization of global security governance is now recognized (Grabosky, 2013; Liss & Sharman, 2015), the precise shape of governance *as* criminalized and securitized compliance *within* organizations and *of* workers, suppliers, customers, and others, particularly in the context of big data and advances in artificial intelligence and machine learning, has so far received little attention. The compliance and RegTech industries supply not only benign compliance, audit, and monitoring systems but also surveillance software and insider threat detection and management systems (INSA, 2018), private investigations, forensic analytics, intelligence solutions, and more, while relying heavily on recruitment from the ranks of former intelligence, police and military officers, and other security personnel. Turning anti-corruption into a matter of national security further legitimizes the widely supported integration of private intelligence contractors into compliance. This logic of intelligence is already built into the technological and algorithmic architectures of the data-driven tools developed by the RegTech industry—background checks, sanctions screening, KYC, due diligence, enhanced due diligence (EDD)—all increasingly rely on privatized intelligence and intelligence products, many automated or semi-automated. Public–private partnerships in national security and intelligence are not only to grow, but to intersect even more deeply with the audit industry at large, with the 'consultocracy' (Ylönen & Kuusela, 2019), now legitimized by an additional good cause, the *securitized* fight against corruption. This is how the pluralization of 'high policing' (Brodeur, 2007) and of intelligence and outsourcing of intelligence functions is both legitimized and accelerated (Keefe, 2010; O'Reilly, 2015).

The regulatory complexity has become such, as the compliance industry experts like to say, that it is beyond human capacity to process all the regulatory requirements. The future well may be one where RegTech (regulatory technologies) fights with SupTech (supervisory technologies), and compliance and 'crime fighting' are effectively automated and delegated to machines; the majority of suspicious activity reports (SARs) from financial institutions received by financial intelligence units are after all already being processed and 'closed' by machines, with a minority selected for human processing. The compliance-industrial complex testifies to nothing less than the explosion of privatization of control which takes a particular form, namely of compliance as governance and management of crime, crime risk, and even security threats—as cybercrime is becoming incorporated into the matrix of compliance; the introduction of the Cyber Incident Reporting for Critical Infrastructure Act of 2022 (CIRCIA) in the United States that requires covered entities in the private sector to report ransom payments and cybersecurity incidents to the Cybersecurity and Infrastructure Security Agency (CISA)[16] is a case in point.

Anti-policies of various kind, from anti-corruption, anti-money laundering, via counter-terrorism measures, sanctions regimes, to counter-radicalization policies (such as the UK Prevent Duty), not only enlist both private and public actors in intelligence gathering for the state but also *delegate* the authority of the state to these actors. Corporations and public sector institutions find themselves in a paradoxical situation where

---

[16] https://www.lawfareblog.com/2022-cyber-incident-reporting-law-key-issues-watch (last accessed May 9, 2022).

increased regulation of their actions simultaneously empowers them—
here we must not let ourselves be fooled by the notion of 'compliance'.
On the one hand, both private and public organizations find themselves,
through the different anti-policies, under the *legal obligation* to comply
and collect certain forms of information which can or do translate into
(state) intelligence, to actively prevent crime and police possible futures
through risk assessments, to fill out suspicious activity reports which
are then passed on to financial intelligence units (Amicelle & Iafolla,
2018), to conduct due diligence typically involving background checks
or internal investigations, to *anticipate* and single out risks and threats
for society, and to inform relevant state authorities. At the same time,
as we have seen, these preventive and predictive intelligence practices,
as well as the proliferation of private investigations, both practices of
private policing and intelligence work, are legitimized through the moral
imperatives of anti-policies, of codes of conduct, of ethics. The problem
is that being predictive, future oriented, and preventive—thus mirroring
the trends towards intelligence-led, predictive, and data-driven policing
(Egbert & Krasmann, 2019; Ferguson, 2017; Fyfe et al., 2018; Joh,
2017; Ratcliffe, 2016)—*compliance takes the form of hybridized and privatized intelligence-led policing*, legitimized by the recourse to morality and
existential threats, for society, for the state and for social order itself in the
context of criminal and foreign policy: corruption, crime, fraud, organized
crime, terrorism, radicalization, sanctions, and so on.

As Tsingou rightly pointed out, AML professionals and compliance
industry actors are to be seen as 'new governors on the block', as 'foot
soldiers in the fight against money laundering' who 'not only implement and monitor' but also 'shape the content of governance', while
engaging in 'regulatory creep', further expanding the regulatory architectures (Tsingou, 2018, p. 69). As Tsingou shows, the professionalization
of compliance went hand in hand with the expansion of the scope of
compliance as governance and with a constant search for ever new areas
to submit to its control. This regulatory creep is also accompanied by a
technological function creep, where new and ever-smaller areas of human
behaviour are being subjected to ever tighter control and coercion built
into the algorithmic architectures under the guise of targeting 'indicators'
and 'early behavioural red flags' which may suggest corrupt, fraudulent,
or otherwise problematic future actions. These opaque control structures
are increasingly hard to challenge, precisely because they are sold in the
name of compliance with anti-policies nobody can be against.

On Regulatory Hybridization and Blurring

As we have seen, the formerly siloed battles are now being integrated into each other, precisely under the umbrella of the *moral* fight against the global evils of corruption, identified both as a symptom and as a cause of many of these global criminal scenarios. This integration of diverse agendas into the same governance logic has necessarily been paralleled by increasing regulatory *hybridization*: by the blurring of boundaries between the public and the private, between policy, law enforcement and implementation, and between regulator and regulated—indeed, with profound consequences for how we are being governed. As anti-policies are increasingly integrated into each other, and as private actors become increasingly enlisted in both their development and execution, we witness hybridization of both global governance and compliance. This hybridization is further accelerated by the insatiable demand for more data—the new oil—and for the *integration* of data sets; the logic of 'new governance' appears to seamlessly align with this hunger for data. As Solomon argued, 'new governance regulation frequently blurs the roles of regulatory actors, the stages of regulation, the modes of regulation, the functions of a regulatory regime; and the structure of the regulatory regime' (Solomon, 2010, p. 591). While this blurring of boundaries is perceived as a strength of these new regulatory approaches in much of the literature on new governance and responsive regulation (Braithwaite, 2008), I refer to this literature solely for its correct observations of this form of regulatory hybridization (Sataøen, 2018), without sharing the same enthusiasm.

Regulatory blurring and hybridization enable the compliance industry to smoothly insert itself into contemporary global crime governance; new governance blurs not only roles but most importantly for us here the 'boundaries between law enforcement, and policy and implementation' (Solomon, 2010, p. 595). It is precisely at the intersection of regulatory hybridization or 'regulatory capitalism' (Levi-Faur, 2017) and 'surveillance capitalism' (Zuboff, 2019) that the compliance-industrial complex has emerged as an increasingly powerful actor in global *governance*; the reliance of compliance on big data and the new possibilities of machine learning and data analytics is not to be underestimated—as is the power it acquired through this data-driven turn. This is something that has allowed it to plug itself into the structures of 'governance by proxy' that have relied on private intelligence agencies and private ICT infrastructures

(Elkin-Koren & Haber, 2016). This regulatory architecture is built, as we saw, around the key notion of risk which precisely lends itself to a technocratic 'governance by numbers' (Supiot, 2017), as the unpredictable futures are reduced to numbers that can be managed, delivering an illusion of control. Tombs and Whyte have rightly observed that responsive regulation 'entrenches a shift towards a risk-based, targeted enforcement approach' (Tombs & Whyte, 2013, p. 62), which gave rise to the now almost omnipresent risk-based (self-)regulation. Risk assessments are at the heart of practical compliance work as well as the work of supervisory authorities (Hansen, 2011). Numbers, indicators, and indexes are endlessly fetishized (Merry, 2020). But while Tombs and Whyte argued that we are dealing with 'a new, institutionalized realpolitik of regulatory regimes from which regulators are absent and any credible threat of enforcement has all but disappeared' (Tombs & Whyte, 2013, p. 75), it is the relatively rare but spectacular and symbolically powerful enforcement actions that stimulate the growth of the compliance-industrial complex. Much like mediated corruption and fraud scandals, terror events, or the 'me-too' movement stimulate the growth of anti-policies, the spectacular enforcement actions, even if rare, stimulate the growth of the compliance-industrial complex. Whether a 'credible threat' or not, they are transformed into another source of risk, 'compliance risks', or rather, risks of non-compliance, such as fines, reputational damage, jailtime, and so on. Or as Deloitte puts it in a blog post titled 'What you don't contain can hurt you', the 'threat posed to a company's financial, organizational, or reputational standing resulting from violations of laws, regulations, codes of conduct, or organizational standards of practice'.[17] Failures—both of enforcement and of the compliance architectures themselves, such as the inability to prevent crime—are therefore not necessarily a problem for the industry. To the contrary, failures and inefficiencies drive the industry as well as regulators forward. While they may not be as successful in the self-declared aims, they do succeed in pushing us away from the world of national sovereignties, rule of law, democracy, and justice and towards global technobureaucratic anticipatory and punitive governance.

While this proliferation of soft and hard regulation, of anti-corruption groups, pledges, treaties, 'co-regulation', and public–private partnerships

[17] https://www2.deloitte.com/us/en/pages/finance/articles/cfo-insights-compliance-risks.html (last accessed August 10, 2022).

has thus fuelled the massive growth of the compliance-industrial complex, the more of this hybridized regulatory architecture we have, the emptier it appears. The more powerful, the more—paradoxically—impotent. Hyper-focused on process, procedure, form, bureaucracy, reporting, audit, and so on, it tends to forget precisely that which it declares to control and quantify. The aforementioned expansion and strategic policy stretching of the concept of 'corruption' has arguably led to the hollowing out of the concept (Bukovansky, 2006), while it has simultaneously gained increased moral and legitimatory force; the emptier and the more hybridized, the more powerful and the more exploitable and versatile—politically and economically.

Taken together, the contemporary governance landscape appears to suffer from an *anti-policy syndrome*, comprising a set of symptoms that run together: (1) moralism, moralizing, and postulations of *moral obligation* to act that legitimize anti-policies but are strikingly unable to achieve moral ends, (2) the *legal obligation* to implement intelligence-led technobureaucratic and technocratic solutions that both delegate the authority of the state to private actors and reduce contentious political issues into a matter of elitist expert-driven and evidence-based 'good governance' prescriptions, (3) overreliance on *particular* forms of expert knowledge and on the reduction of the social and the political to quantified indicators, rankings, benchmarking, standardization, perpetual assessments, and other feats of managerial engineering (Merry, 2011), (4) the simultaneous cultivation of 'technosolutionism' (Morozov, 2013), where these complex social issues become further reduced to even tinier technical problems that can be optimized and tweaked using the right algorithm, platform or app, and decisions automated, (5) the cultivation of empty forms of (deontological) 'ethics', 'ethical guidelines', and postulations of 'values' such as integrity and transparency, which are in practice reduced to a form of accounting (e.g. integrity indicators), (6) the never-ceasing regulatory activity and regulatory hybridization that stimulates the proliferation of complex and obscure structures of delegation and governance by proxy which enable evasions of responsibility, and fuel unaccountability and 'new corruption' that are as a rule conveniently invisible to the technobureaucratic gaze, as Wedel has convincingly argued (Wedel, 2014), (7) the securitization and 'criminalization' of an ever greater range of phenomena, and the simultaneous implementation of systems that *imitate* or *simulate* the logic of the criminal justice system, and finally, (8) the drive towards anticipatory forms of governance and a 'pre-crime society' (Arrigo & Sellers, 2021), where securitized risks and threats are to be tackled before they materialize. This anti-policy syndrome materializes itself precisely in the expansion of particular forms of control architectures that rely on and are legitimized through anti-policies and that demand *compliance* as a solution, which also happens to be a big business. Due to the regulatory hybridization and the increasing complexity of multi-layered, proxy, delegated, and distributed governance structures, we often find ourselves unable to make explicit sense of the changing modes of control we are subjected and interpellated by. But it should be clear by now that anti-policies are in practice fuelling the privatization of control and policing, diverting resources into compliance, internal control, conduct risk management, monitoring, surveillance, and intelligence gathering in the name of prevention, anticipation, prediction, risk management, and threat detection, with the goal of their handling and/or elimination. We should also pause and think about the peculiarity of translating anti-policies driven by moral outrage and scandals into ritualized technobureaucratic practices as a hegemonic mode of securitized governance.

The war in Ukraine, ongoing at the time of writing, is further accelerating this process of regulatory hybridization and intensifying the reliance on securitized compliance as a solution to the world's most pressing problems. We have seen the imposition of unprecedented sanctions packages targeting Russian oligarchs and kleptocrats and the Russian economy, which has given a massive boost to the compliance-industrial complex, to the global fight against corruption, and to its further integration into the security establishment and surveillance-industrial complex. Indeed, only shortly after the launch of this strategy, the war in Ukraine has actualized this securitization of anti-corruption; United States and its Western partners have targeted sanctions and asset freezes at corrupt senior officials, oligarchs, and other high-ranking Russian elites, cracked down on their wealth, and on the symbolically powerful luxury real estate enclaves which had until then been tolerated, on their luxury yachts and private jets,[18] and the elites' 'golden passports', all of which have long secured the privileged mobilities of the ultra-rich and the kleptocrats (Shachar, 2018). As Biden put it, they 'share the corrupt gains of the Kremlin policies, and

---

[18] https://www.news.com.au/finance/money/wealth/were-coming-for-you-biden-says-us-will-seize-russian-oligarchs-yachts-apartments-private-jets/news-story/5de60e2d4 8a244a9284608da8c9fb1ba (last accessed March 11, 2022).

should share in the pain as well'.[19] Commentators have already remarked that the war has 'turbo-charged the anti-corruption efforts'[20] and that something good may come out of this after all, since 'a crackdown on the oligarchs could also offer solutions to broader social problems. Increased regulation of hidden assets and blind trusts would address the growing plague of political corruption that is evident in the U.S. and elsewhere'.[21] Simultaneously, new threat assessments from Western financial crime units warned of the increased risks of corruption and money laundering in many countries due to the war and the related disruption of supply chains, as well as increased threat of other transnational organized crimes, human trafficking, and so forth.[22] What is less talked about is the fact that causing this 'pain' and responding to new corruption and even organized crime threats is to a large degree outsourced to the compliance-industrial complex. While it is beyond the scope of this short book to discuss the effects of the expansion of the sanctions regimes, the unfolding war makes a critical understanding of global crime governance and the fight against corruption even more timely. And the integration of sanctions regimes with anti-corruption further testifies to the thesis of regulatory hybridization and the move towards integrated, platform-like solutions. Updated sanctions screening tools are smoothly integrated in pre-existing offerings of consultancy firms; as an example, we may take a promotional message from FTI Consulting and its 'Anti-Money Laundering, Sanctions & Anti-corruption Solutions', which taken together captures well the trends in the industry:

> Our professionals offer comprehensive solutions to financial institutions and other organizations facing unprecedented scrutiny and pressure to serve as the first line of defense in the global war on money laundering

[19] https://www.bbc.com/news/world-europe-60488037, BBC News, February 23, 2022 (last accessed February 24, 2022).

[20] https://www.politico.com/news/2022/03/07/russia-war-ukraine-anti-corruption-00014532 (last accessed March 16, 2022).

[21] https://www.theatlantic.com/ideas/archive/2022/02/russia-sanctions-punish-rich-oligarchs/622933/ (last accessed March 1, 2022).

[22] A case in point is the 2022 threat assessment by Økokrim, the *National Authority for Investigation and Prosecution of Economic and Environmental Crime*, which lists a range of new and heightened corruptions threats as a consequence of the war in Ukraine: https://www.okokrim.no/oekokrims-trusselvurdering-2022.6527255-549350.html (last accessed May 2, 2022).

and terrorist financing. Clients benefit from our world-renowned expertise and cutting-edge technical capabilities (...) FTI Consulting is well positioned to assist you with all aspects of your organization's compliance, risk management and investigations efforts. We offer end-to-end anti-money laundering, sanctions and anti-corruption consulting services. (...) FTI Consulting's technology and large-scale data analysis expertise complements our investigative and compliance expertise to help entities develop effective compliance, detection, and risk management programs. (...) FTI Consulting develops and assesses comprehensive compliance programs, including key components such as compliance structure, policies and procedures, risk assessments, control effectiveness, training and governance. We help ensure that the compliance programs of our clients account for the risk factors relevant to their specific institutions and establish sound policies and procedures, effective controls and a strong governance structure. (...) FTI Consulting leverages our team of former bank regulators, law enforcement personnel, and industry professionals to support clients that have come under regulatory or law enforcement scrutiny. Our professionals regularly appear before regulatory and law enforcement bodies on important matters such as enforcement activity, rulemaking, and industry trends. Many of our professionals have been qualified as AML experts by state and federal courts. By ensuring that governance, control, and risk management structures are firmly in place and operating effectively, we help our clients meet the challenges of complying with ever-evolving regulations and avoid regulatory, law enforcement, and reputational "hot buttons." (...) FTI Investigations, our in-house private investigations agency, has unmatched expertise in the search, synthesis and analysis of information from public and non-public sources. We act quickly and discreetly to provide our clients with the essential information necessary to make key decisions concerning their counterparties, clients, vendors and other associates.[23]

The expansion of the sanctions regimes thus merely magnified and made visible trends that pre-date the war and that are at the core of the rise of the compliance-industrial complex as shall be discussed throughout this book: (1) the *securitization* of anti-corruption and its *deeper integration* into related regulatory modalities of fighting transnational crimes, (2) the dependence of the effectiveness of these regulations on governments' ability to obtain *compliance of* the private sector and the sectors enforcement of *internal compliance regimes* (Early, 2021), and hence (3)

---

[23] https://www.fticonsulting.com/~/media/Files/us-files/insights/brochure/anti-money-laundering-sanctions-corruption-solutions.pdf (last accessed August 2, 2022).

the key *policing* and *pre-crime* role of the compliance, private financial investigative agencies and private intelligence industry actors, compliance departments, and other industry experts who execute these orders and who are responsible for ensuring compliance, conducting due diligence and risk assessments, and investigations, and, finally, (4) the growing role of data-driven tools, analytics, and artificial intelligence in compliance, or else, of RegTech (regulatory technologies), including in sanctions screening, KYC (know your customer), suspicious activity reporting, and (enhanced) due diligence, which push a more predictive and pre-emptive logic, and (5) the emphasis placed on monitoring and accounting for ethics and compliance culture, as well as prediction of ethical breaches. In the next chapter, we will build on these insights in an attempt to bring to light the nature of the compliance-industrial complex.

REFERENCES

Althusser, L. (1971). Ideology and ideological state apparatuses. In t. B. Brewster (Ed.), *Lenin and philosophy, and other essays* (pp. 127–188). New Left Books.

Amicelle, A., & Iafolla, V. (2018). Suspicion-in-the-making: Surveillance and denunciation in financial policing. *The British Journal of Criminology, 58*(4), 845–863. https://doi.org/10.1093/bjc/azx051

Aradau, C., & van Munster, R. (2007). Governing terrorism through risk: Taking precautions, (un)knowing the future. *European Journal of International Relations, 13*(1), 89–115. https://doi.org/10.1177/1354066610707 4290

Arrigo, B., & Sellers, B. (Eds.). (2021). *The pre-crime society: Crime, culture and control in the ultramodern age*. Bristol University Press. https://doi.org/10.1332/policypress/9781529205251.001.0001

Bigo, D. (2002). Security and immigration: Toward a critique of the governmentality of unease. *Alternatives, 27*, 63–92. https://doi.org/10.1177/030 437540202700S105

Braithwaite, J. (2008). *Regulatory capitalism: How it works, ideas for making it better*. Edward Elgar. https://doi.org/10.4337/9781848441262

Brodeur, J.-P. (2007). High and low policing in post-9/11 times. *Policing, 1*(1), 25–37. https://doi.org/10.1093/police/pam002

Bukovansky, M. (2006). The hollowness of anti-corruption discourse. *Review of International Political Economy, 13*(2), 181–209. https://doi.org/10.1080/09692290600625413

Campbell-Verduyn, M., Goguen, M., & Porter, T. (2017). Big Data and algorithmic governance: The case of financial practices. *New Political Economy, 22*(2), 219–236. https://doi.org/10.1080/13563467.2016.1216533

Early, B. R. (2021). Making sanctions work: Promoting compliance, punishing violations, and discouraging sanctions busting. In P. A. G. van Bergeijk (Ed.), *Research handbook on economic sanctions*. Edward Elgar. https://doi.org/10.4337/9781839102721.00015

Egbert, S., & Krasmann, S. (2019). Predictive policing: Not yet, but soon preemptive? *Policing and Society, 30*(8), 905–919. https://doi.org/10.1080/10439463.2009.1611821

Elkin-Koren, N., & Haber, E. (2016). Governance by proxy: Cyber challenges to civil liberties. *Brooklyn Law Review, 82*, 105–162.

Ferguson, A. G. (2017). *The rise of big data policing: Surveillance, race, and the future of law enforcement*. New York University Press. https://doi.org/10.2307/j.ctt1pwtb27

Fyfe, N., Gundhus, H., & Rønn, K. V. (Eds.). (2018). *Moral issues in intelligence-led policing*. Routledge. https://doi.org/10.4324/9781315231259

Grabosky, P. (2013). Beyond responsive regulation: The expanding role of non-state actors in the regulatory process. *Regulation & Governance, 7*, 114–123. https://doi.org/10.1111/j.1748-5991.2012.01147.x

Graeber, D. (2018). *Bullshit jobs: A theory*. Simon & Schuster.

Hansen, H. K. (2011). Managing corruption risks. *Review of International Political Economy, 18*(2), 251–275. https://doi.org/10.1080/09692291003791448

Hansen, H. K., & Tang-Jensen, M. H. (2015). Making up corruption control: Conducting due diligence in a Danish law firm. *Ephemera: Theory & Politics in Organization, 15*(2), 365–385.

Haugh, T. (2017). The criminalization of compliance. *Notre Dame Law Review, 92*(3), 1215–1270.

INSA. (2018). *Assessing the mind of the malicious insider: Using a behavioral model and data analytics to improve continuous evaluation*. https://www.insaonline.org/wp-content/uploads/2017/04/INSA_WP_Mind_Insider_FIN.pdf

Jakobi, A. P. (2017). Global norms and US foreign policy change: The governance of transnational crime. *International Politics, 54*, 683–697. https://doi.org/10.1057/s41311-017-0059-3

Joh, E. E. (2017). Artificial intelligence and policing: First questions. *Seattle University Law Review, 41*, 1139–1144.

Johns, F. (2017). Data mining as governance. In R. Brownsword, E. Scotford, & K. Yeung (Eds.), *The Oxford handbook of law, regulation and technology*. Oxford University Press. https://doi.org/10.1093/oxfordhb/9780199680832.013.56

Kajsiu, B. (2021). Public or private corruption? The ideological dimension of anti-corruption discourses in Colombia, Ecuador and Albania. *Journal of Extreme Anthropology, 5*(2), 27–51. https://doi.org/10.5617/jea.9243

Kaleem, A. (2022). Citizen-led intelligence gathering under UK's prevent duty. In H. Ben Jaffel & S. Larsson (Eds.), *Problematising intelligence studies: Towards a new research agenda* (pp. 73–95). Routledge. https://doi.org/10.4324/9781003205463-6

Kalpokas, I. (2019). *Algorithmic governance: Politics and law in the post-human era.* Palgrave Macmillan. https://doi.org/10.1007/978-3-030-31922-9

Katzarova, E. (2019). *The social construction of global corruption: From utopia to neoliberalism.* Palgrave Macmillan. https://doi.org/10.1007/978-3-319-985 69-5

Katzenbach, C., & Ulbricht, L. (2019). Algorithmic governance. *Internet Policy Review, 8*(4), 1–18. https://doi.org/10.14763/2019.4.1424

Keefe, P. R. (2010). Privatized spying: The emerging intelligence industry. In L. K. Johnson (Ed.), *The Oxford handbook of national security intelligence* (pp. 297–310). Oxford University Press. https://doi.org/10.1093/oxfordhb/9780195375886.003.0018

Kuldova, T. Ø. (2019). Fetishism and the problem of disavowal. *Qualitative Market Research.* https://doi.org/10.1108/QMR-12-2016-0125

Lakoff, G., & Johnson, M. (2003). *Metaphors we live by.* University of Chicago Press. https://doi.org/10.7208/chicago/9780226470993.001.0001

Levi-Faur, D. (2017). Regulatory capitalism. In P. Drahos (Ed.), *Regulatory theory: Foundation and applications* (pp. 289–302). ANU Press. https://doi.org/10.22459/RT.02.2017.17

Liss, C., & Sharman, J. C. (2015). Global corporate crime-fighters: Private transnational responses to piracy and money laundering. *Review of International Political Economy, 22*(4), 693–718. https://doi.org/10.1080/09692290.2014.936482

Lordon, F. (2014). *Willing slaves of capital: Spinoza & Marx on desire.* Verso.

MacIntyre, A. (2007). *After virtue: A study in moral theory.* University of Notre Dame Press.

McGoey, L. (2019). *Unknowers: How strategic ignorance rules the world.* ZED Books. https://doi.org/10.5040/9781350225725

Merry, S. E. (2011). Measuring the world: Indicators, human rights, and global governance. *Current Anthropology, 52*, S83–S95. https://doi.org/10.1086/657241

Merry, S. E. (2020). The problem of compliance and the turn to quantification. In M.-C. Foblets, M. Goodale, M. Sapignoli, & O. Zenker (Eds.), *The Oxford handbook of law and anthropology.* Oxford University Press. https://doi.org/10.1093/oxfordhb/9780198840534.013.43

Morozov, E. (2013). *To save everything, click here.* Public Affairs.

Mungiu-Pippidi, A. (2021). The universalization of ethical universalism. In A. Bågenholm, M. Bauhr, M. Grimes, & B. Rothstein (Eds.), *The Oxford handbook of quality government* (pp. 26–42). Oxford University Press. https://doi.org/10.1093/oxfordhb/9780198858218.013.3

Newburn, T., & Jones, T. (2007). Symbolizing crime control: Reflections on zero tolerance. *Theoretical Criminology, 11*(2), 221–243. https://doi.org/10.1177/1362480607075849

O'Reilly, C. (2015). The pluralization of high policing: Convergence and divergence at the public-private interface. *British Journal of Criminology, 55*(4), 688–710. https://doi.org/10.1093/bjc/azu114

OECD. (2019). *Analytics for integrity: Data-driven approaches for enhancing corruption and fraud risk assessments.* OECD.

Østbø, J. (2017). Securitizing "spiritual-moral values" in Russia. *Post-Soviet Affairs, 33*(3), 200–216. https://doi.org/10.1080/1060586X.2016.1251023

Ratcliffe, J. H. (2016). *Intelligence-led policing.* Routledge.

Sataøen, H. L. (2018). Regulokratene: Den nye styringsprofesjonen? *Norsk sosiologisk tidsskrift, 2*(6), 481–499. https://doi.org/10.18261/issn.2535-2512-2018-06-03

Scott, B. (2022). *Cloudmoney: Cash, cards, crypto, and the war for our wallets.* HarperCollins.

Shachar, A. (2018). Dangerous liaisons: Money and citizenship. In R. Bauböck (Ed.), *Debating transformations of national citizenship* (pp. 7–15). Springer. https://doi.org/10.1007/978-3-319-92719-0_2

Shore, C. (2008). Audit culture and liberal governance: Universities and the politics of accountability. *Anthropological Theory, 8*(3), 278–298. https://doi.org/10.1177/1463499608093815

Shore, C., & Wright, S. (2015). Audit culture revisited: Rankings, ratings, and the reassembling of society. *Current Anthropology, 56*(3), 421–444. https://doi.org/10.1086/681534

Silverman, K. (2016). Male subjectivity at the margins. *Routledge.* https://doi.org/10.4324/9780203699676

Solomon, J. M. (2010). New governance, preemptive self-regulation, and the blurring of boundaries in regulatory theory and practice. *Wisconsin Law Review, 2010*(2), 591–625.

Supiot, A. (2017). *Governance by numbers: The making of a legal model of allegiance.* Bloomsbury.

Tombs, S., & Whyte, D. (2013). Transcending the deregulation debate? Regulation, risk, and the enforcement of health and safety law in the UK. *Regulation & Governance, 7*, 61–79. https://doi.org/10.1111/j.1748-5991.2012.01164.x

Tsingou, E. (2018). New governors on the block: The rise of anti-money laundering professionals. *Crime, Law and Social Change, 69*, 191–205. https://doi.org/10.1007/s10611-017-9751-x

Walters, W. (2008). Anti-policy and anti-politics: Critical reflections on certain schemes to govern bad things. *European Journal of Cultural Studies, 11*(3), 267–288. https://doi.org/10.1177/1367549408091844

Wathne, C., & Stephenson, M. C. (2021). *The credibility of corruption statistics: A critical review of ten global estimates.* U4. https://www.u4.no/publicati ons/the-credibility-of-corruption-statistics.pdf

Wedel, J. (2014). *How the establishment corrupted our finances, freedom and politics and created an outsider class.* Pegasus Books.

Wolf, M. (2003). The morality of the market. *Foreign Policy, 138*, 46–50. https://doi.org/10.2307/3183655

Ylönen, M., & Kuusela, H. (2019). Consultocracy and its discontents: A critical typology and a call for a research agenda. *Governance, 32*, 241–258. https://doi.org/10.1111/gove.12369

Žižek, S. (1989). *The sublime object of ideology.* Verso.

Zuboff, S. (2019). *The age of surveillance capitalism: The fight for a human future at the new frontier of power.* Profile Books.

CHAPTER 3

The Compliance-Industrial Complex

Abstract We transition from the world of anti-policies into the realm of the compliance-industrial complex. We explore its relation to the security-industrial complex and military-industrial complex, and we flesh out the core argument of this book. Namely, that we are currently witness to the emergence of criminalized and securitized data-driven and intelligence-led compliance as a new hybrid mode of governance that instrumentalizes hollow notions of ethics and ethical compliance 'cultures'—all legitimized by the global fight against corruption and transnational organized crime. We begin to delve into the world of RegTech (regulatory technologies) and take on the ways in which compliance enhances corporate sovereignty rather than setting limits to it and we ponder the transformation of social control under neoliberalism.

Keywords Compliance-industrial complex · Pluralization of policing · Intelligence-led compliance · Corporate sovereignty · RegTech · Pre-crime society

The concept of the *compliance-industrial complex* as hinted at earlier aims to capture the power apparatus that has emerged at the nexus of global crime governance and regulation by governments, private and voluntary regulation, the 'consultocracy' (Ylönen & Kuusela, 2019),

47

T. Ø. Kuldova, *Compliance-Industrial Complex*,
https://doi.org/10.1007/978-3-031-19224-1_3

and the tech industry—or else, at the nexus of 'regulatory capitalism' (Levi-Faur, 2017) and 'surveillance capitalism' (Zuboff, 2019). The compliance-industrial complex emerged in response to anti-corruption and anti-money laundering policies since the 1990s, and with the parallel turn to 'corporate ethics'. Over time, it has largely managed to monopolize and standardize the narrative, policies, regulatory instruments, and solutions designed to fight or rather pre-empt these crimes. The growth of this compliance-industrial complex owes to the rise of regulatory capitalism, global governance, and the proliferation regulatory instruments in tandem with internal control legislation which has *de facto* delegated state powers, at least partially, to private actors; 'regulatory states' have thus created these markets and stimulated their growth in tandem with multilateral and transnational private regulations (Levi-Faur, 2017; Veggeland, 2009, 2010). The concept of the compliance-industrial complex helps us think this transformation of governance, as it sketches the broad contours of a multi-billion-dollar industry invested in translating (and stimulating more) governmental regulation into governance products that ensure and often also exceed mere legal compliance. This industry is projected to grow rapidly in the next decade: the global enterprise governance, risk, and compliance market was valued at USD 35.1 billion in 2020[1] and forecasted to reach USD 97.3 billion by 2028[2] while the governance, risk, and compliance *platform* market was projected to reach USD 68.7 billion by 2027[3] and the RegTech market was 'valued at USD 15.68 billion in 2020 and is projected to reach USD 87.17 billion by 2028'.[4] These estimates may indeed overlap as the distinctions and categories are far from straightforward, the can even be exaggerated, but it is fair to say that the industry is *perceived* as a booming market. As one of my informants put it, with a hint of cynicism in his voice, the industry is driven

---

[1] https://www.prnewswire.com/news-releases/enterprise-governance-risk--compliance-market-size-worth-96-98-billion-by-2028--cagr-14-1--polaris-market-research-301432800.html (last accessed April 20, 2022).

[2] https://www.grandviewresearch.com/press-release/global-enterprise-governance-risk-compliance-egrc-market (last accessed April 20, 2022).

[3] https://www.imarcgroup.com/governance-risk-compliance-platform-market (last accessed April 20, 2022).

[4] https://www.prnewswire.com/news-releases/regtech-market-size-worth--87-17-billion-globally-by-2028-at-23-92-cagr-verified-market-research-301497770.html (last accessed April 20, 2022).

by a 'vicious circle of regulation and innovation (…) it will grow, without changing anything, only adding more control mechanisms, but these too won't be enough, so it will grow more (…) it is a really good business to be in'.

The compliance-industrial complex is, for obvious reasons—such as the fight against transnational crime—intertwined in particular with what has been described as the 'surveillance-industrial complex' (Hayes, 2012) and to a certain degree also the 'military-industrial complex' (Roland, 2007). It can be argued that it has much of the same corrosive effect 'on political culture, democratic governance and social control' (Hayes, 2012, p. 167). But while the state-corporate networks of surveillance and intelligence actors are indeed being increasingly well integrated into compliance, providing key elements of the compliance solutions, compliance is significant in that it has become a form of governance that also seeks to dictate our values and ethics, it is a mode of social control and one of the leading ways in which governments and multilateral organizations seek to address global challenges. Surveillance and intelligence then come in service of compliance *as* governance, and in service of enforcement of values and 'ethical cultures'. While both the military-industrial and the surveillance-industrial complex received much attention, the compliance-industrial complex has been so far largely ignored by critical researchers. And yet, it is here that regulations, standards, guidelines, directives, and so forth are both shaped and translated into concrete compliance products and services that subject workers, suppliers, citizens, and others to different forms of control, scrutiny, and sanctions.

On Scandals

The fear of fines and reputational damage, the spectacular corruption, corporate and accounting scandals, and financial revelations such as the Panama Papers, Pandora Papers, LuxLeaks, Dubai Leaks, or FinCen Files, have all fuelled both regulatory activities and the global expansion and implementation of compliance regimes—paradoxically, by the same compliance and audit industry actors that have been routinely found implicated in these scandals as both professional facilitators and beneficiaries. Scandals serve the moral renewal and regeneration of societies (Baudrillard, 1994); but the inflation of these scandals, even their simulation, manufacturing, hyper-mediation, and indulgence in their consumption, may point to a society of moral confusion, one that simultaneously searches for its own morality, while delegating its moral outrage to these scandals only to continue with business as usual. The moral judgements accompanying scandals which drive anti-policies are conspicuously lacking in the technobureaucratic solutions which are introduced in their aftermath, such as risk assessments that sacrifice morality at the altar of simulated objectivity, denying the obvious—that every risk assessment is a result of discretionary judgement. In this sense, the scandal appears to periodically reproduce the system as is, or even increase the power of its institutions. Rather than 'shaking it up', it helps to maintain its moral façade.

These numerous corruption and corporate and accounting scandals—and of course events such as 9/11, the financial crisis of 2008, the COVID-19 pandemic, and now the war in Ukraine—have all stimulated the growth of increasingly complex technocratic regulations, directives, and guidelines. These instruments typically seek to regulate and monitor *internal control and compliance systems*—as opposed to the reality on ground. They ask whether systems and procedures are in place, and for supporting bureaucratic documentation, the proof of their existence, rather than being concerned with investigating the realities on the ground; the focus is shifted to the control of (internal) control, where the latter becomes a proxy for reality. This need for a proof has also contributed to the expansion of the market for data-driven compliance solutions. Regulation that comes into place following scandals often demands precisely this sort of internal control: from the US Foreign Corrupt Practices Act or FCPA from 1977—criminalizing bribery of foreign public officials, following the investigations by the U.S. Securities and Exchange Commission into bribery of foreign officials by over 400 U.S. companies, most notably Lockheed, the Sarbanes–Oxley Act (SOX) from 2002 written following the scandals in companies such as Enron, WorldCom, Tyco International, or Adelphia which made 'good corporate governance' a federal law, to the UK Global Anti-Corruption Sanctions Regime from 2021, written in response to global corruption scandals and with the intention to sanction corrupt individuals. FCPA and SOX have increased the threat of individual and corporate criminal and civil penalties, this again contributed to the growth of the compliance function, internal controls, and risk-based approaches.

The primary innovation of SOX is its insistence that individual business leaders personally attest to the validity of the financial reporting they are presenting to shareholders, with the threat of personal criminal liability hanging over their heads for non-compliance. No wonder the law has received such laser sharp focus from top managers. (Taylor, 2006, p. xix)

And this is not to mention a whole range of other acts, multilateral agreements, directives, guidelines, standards, voluntary codes of conduct, and so forth, which, too, have typically emerged in response to different scandals and revelations and which, too, urge the implementation of risk-based approaches.

ON THE SHIFT FROM LEGAL COMPLIANCE TO ETHICAL COMPLIANCE CULTURES

The compliance-industrial complex shapes the forms that surveillance takes and the ways in which it becomes utilized in *practice*—in the name of governance, social control, and the implementation of anti-policies and visions of greater good. As such, the compliance products and services that flood the market are ideological—first and foremost in their materiality and in the practices and actions that stem from them (Althusser, 1971). This is why also these products deserve closer scrutiny, as prime sites of the translation of governance and regulation into practice, one that increasingly and often almost invisibly subjects us. What an analysis of both these products and regulatory imperatives reveals is that there has been a shift away from the pursuit of mere legal compliance (the much criticized 'box-ticking' exercise) to attempts to embed ethical compliance cultures in organizations. This embedding, however, much in line with the technobureaucratic logic and the promises of technosolutionism, takes the form of data-driven tools, of quantified assessments of culture which, again, promise to reveal potential 'compliance risks' within organizational cultures. What emerges is a peculiar understanding of 'ethical culture', where the dream is to tap into the potential of its informality, but where the reality is one of its further formalization and dissection into ever-smaller cultural and psycho-social indicators to be managed and manipulated.

At the beginning of Michael Volkov's influential podcast *Corruption, Crime & Compliance*, we can hear the following word from the sponsor, Diligent,[5] which nicely captures both the repetitive nature of these promises and the re-framing of the fight against crime into a matter of increasingly automated risk management and ethics:

> Diligent is the time-tested award-winning provider of automated governance, risk, and compliance solutions. For over 20 years Diligent has helped boards and C-suites to design and implement effective governance practices through its market-leading board application. Diligent has now expanded its offerings to include risk, compliance, and audit solutions. Building on these new and exciting capabilities, Diligent now offers the critical capability to connect boards, C-suite, risk, compliance, and audit teams to promote purpose-driven leadership. Building on this capability, Diligent provides a full suite of complementary services, including risk management, ethics and compliance, environmental, social and governance (ESG), and proactive auditing strategies and practices. Diligent solutions enable companies to implement robust corporate governance to mitigate and manage risk, create a culture of ethics and compliance, ensure that company controls are audit ready and implement tailored and responsive ESG solutions.[6]

The compliance function has evolved from a small and often neglected legal department into a *governance function* that is to—ideally—permeate the whole organization. Or that is at least how the Department of Justice (DOJ) envisions[7] effective corporate compliance programs and defines these in the *Federal Sentencing Guidelines*,[8] when it expects investments into 'compliance culture'. This focus on compliance culture has been reinforced following the notorious Siemens bribery scandal which resulted in $1.6 billion fine to settle the allegations by US and European authorities. In the press release of the Security and Exchange Commission (SEC) from 2008, we can thus read the following,

> The SEC's complaint alleges that between March 12, 2001, and Sept. 30, 2007, Siemens created elaborate payment schemes to conceal the nature

---

[5] https://www.diligent.com/ (last accessed July 29, 2022).

[6] https://blog.volkovlaw.com/2022/07/episode-240-the-ccos-role-in-an-effective-compliance-program/ (last accessed July 29, 2022).

[7] https://www.justice.gov/criminal-fraud/page/file/937501/download (last accessed May 4, 2022).

[8] https://guidelines.ussc.gov/gl/%C2%A78B2.1 (last accessed March 15, 2022).

of its corrupt payments, and the company's inadequate internal controls allowed the conduct to flourish (...) The misconduct involved employees at all levels, including former senior management, and revealed a corporate culture long at odds with the FCPA. The SEC's complaint alleges that despite the company's knowledge of bribery at two of its largest groups — Communications and Power Generation — the tone at the top at Siemens was inconsistent with an effective FCPA compliance program and created a corporate culture in which bribery was tolerated and even rewarded at the highest levels of the company.[9]

The DOJs charging papers similarly alleged that Siemens' compliance program existed only on the paper, in addition to pervasive practices of falsification of corporate books and records and of evasion of internal control systems,

> Over the period from in or about February 1999 to in or about July 2004, certain SIEMENS ZV members became aware of changes in the regulatory environment. While foreign anti-corruption circulars and policies were promulgated, that "paper program" was largely ineffective at changing SIEMENS' historical, pervasive corrupt business practices.[10]

This intensified the shift towards compliance culture, backed by trainings and control. Compliance is to go beyond mere legal compliance and stretch into the domain of integrity management, culture, and ethics. Enforcement of 'compliance procedures, using disciplinary measures and all reasonable steps to *correct, prevent, and detect future violations*', is central, but so is the focus on compliance culture, values, and ethics. Key is also the 'tone from the top' and the ability to demonstrate the commitment of senior management. The existence, at the time of offence, of such defined 'effective' compliance program that combines internal policing with a program that promotes '*organizational cultures that encourage*

---

[9] https://www.sec.gov/news/press/2008/2008-294.htm (last accessed August 10, 2022).

[10] https://www.justice.gov/sites/default/files/criminal-fraud/legacy/2013/05/02/12-12-08siemensakt-info.pdf (last accessed August 10, 2022).

ethical conduct'[11] or else, a 'culture of compliance'[12] amounts to penalty reductions and reduced sentence; the absence 'can multiply fines up to 400 percent' (Lobel, 2012, p. 75). While these guidelines pertain to US territory, and few other jurisdictions offer sentence reductions tied to compliance systems, they have nonetheless become influential globally, becoming a form of expected standard.

The ISO 37301:2021 *Compliance Management Systems* translates this guidance into its own language and makes compliance, again, penetrate the whole organization, turning it explicitly into a *management* function. In the industry language, compliance is now coming from the top and becoming a part of the 'DNA of the organization'. This development was touted by Volkov Law Group CEO Michael Volkov as 'the biggest revolution in corporate governance'.[13]

ON COMPLIANCE AS PRE-EMPTIVE INTELLIGENCE-LED GOVERNANCE

The evolution of corporate prosecutions over the last two decades with the proliferation of deferred prosecution agreements and non-prosecution agreements and introduction of court-appointed 'compliance monitors' and rewards for those with 'effective' compliance systems in place (Garrett, 2014) have further stimulated the growth of compliance—even to the point of introduction of *pre-emptive* voluntary compliance monitors. This logic of *pre-emption* (McCulloch & Wilson, 2016) is again reinforced by the introduction of predictive technologies that are being embraced in the compliance space and developed by RegTechs in the name of proactive monitoring and anticipation of both internal and external risks and threats. While the US legal system differs in this respect from most other jurisdictions, there is no doubt that compliance products globally are first and foremost developed in alignment with the US system, while regulations in other jurisdictions are added, more or less, on top of this logic.

[11] https://guidelines.ussc.gov/gl/%C2%A78B2.1 (last accessed March 15, 2022; emphasis mine).

[12] https://www.justice.gov/criminal-fraud/page/file/937501/download (last accessed April 29, 2022).

[13] https://member.regtechanalyst.com/corporate-governance-might-be-going-through-its-biggest-ever-revolution/ (last accessed March 1, 2022).

Compliance is in other words effectively to become the operating system of organizations; the issue is that this sort of management takes, more often than not, the form of 'pre-crime' (Arrigo & Sellers, 2021; Hansen, 2018; McCulloch & Wilson, 2016; Zedner, 2007), encompassing even workplace surveillance, and of governance *through* corporate security (Walby & Lippert, 2014), private investigations, and thus privatized justice. One can contemplate here the historical trajectory of the notorious Pinkerton detective agency: from conducting espionage during the Civil War, inspiring the development of agencies such as FBI, Secret Service, or CIA, via union busting, worker intimidation and infiltrations of the labour movement, or else being the hired security goons for the protection of capital, to becoming a global security and risk management firm, a subsidiary of Securitas AB (O'Hara, 2016). Today, Pinkerton is selling its Crime Index, its Risk Wheel, its 'holistic approach to risk and security management', its intelligence services and more.[14] The rogue practices of the Pinkerton spies, mercenaries, and thugs, it could be argued, have not really gone away; rather, they appear to have been rebranded, refined, polished, even made compliant, and perfectly legal, while still protecting and securing the power and interests of capital— labour unions have merely been rebranded as 'workforce risk' (Weiss, 2008).

Compliance has thus not only become a hybridized form of governance but also a form of *managerial control* (Nelson, 2021) that *imitates* the criminal justice system—albeit without the same separation of powers, guarantees of due process and public oversight—while also imitating the knowledge production of intelligence agencies and security establishment. This emergence of compliance as governance is thus a result of the hybridization of regulation, governance, and self-regulation and the simultaneous privatization and pluralization of policing and intelligence. Compliance has *de facto* evolved into an internal intelligence and policing function with expanding operational mandate and scope. Loader was right when he noted that 'novel policing forms are fast outstripping the capacity of existing institutional arrangements to monitor and control them' (Loader, 2000, p. 324). The compliance-industrial complex has become an important player not only in global governance of crime but also in 'moral regulation' (Hunt, 1999), both of which take on an increasingly

[14] https://pinkerton.com/our-insights/blog/holistic-security-the-risk-wheel   (last accessed August 2, 2022).

punitive, datafied, and formalized form—encoded in the ever-proliferating 'best practice' guidelines and systems that rely on principles of (quantified) auditing, accounting, monitoring, and reporting. The consequences of delegating policing and crime fighting functions to compliance and of enlisting corporations and organizations in the fight against corruption, financial crime, human rights abuses, and more *through* systematic work with internal and external threat prevention, risk management, and corporate security systems are rarely explicitly discussed.

ON INTELLIGENCE-LED COMPLIANCE AS A ROUTE TO CORPORATE SOVEREIGNTY

As we have seen earlier, anti-policies create not only a legal obligation to comply, but also a moral obligation. This moral obligation or rather this morality, in turn, is what in practice (also) becomes policed: breaches of ethical codes of conduct are investigated and pre-empted and so on. The expansion of the legitimate role of compliance, however, simultaneously endows both compliance and corporations and other organizations with disproportionate managerial power. It is not a coincidence that we are seeing a trend towards tighter and closer co-operation between compliance and human resources (HR) (Mamaysky, 2021); compliance, by being extended from mere legal compliance into the realm of ethics (thus mirroring the logics of anti-policies), is becoming new iteration of managerial power, a power to control workers, clients, students, suppliers, families, and others; to submit them to excessive monitoring and surveillance (in the name of the good), to the gaze of the *intelligence* analyst—to see them as always already a potential threat, a security risk, a suspicious actor to be evaluated, managed, and eliminated. It is here that we must truly appreciate the key role of private *intelligence* enlisted in the service of the state and its consequences in practice.

While we could mistakenly imagine compliance as a form of *submission* to the state, to the proliferating regulations, this would be to miss that it is, paradoxically, through this act of submission that the authority and the power of the state are delegated onto corporation and organizations, who thus acquire part of the state's *sovereignty*. Moreover, since the form of policing that compliance becomes is best understood as privatized 'high policing', or predominantly as intelligence, it is worth reminding ourselves of the difference between 'low policing', associated with conventional police forces, and 'high policing' as executed by the intelligence services—even if with the rise of intelligence-led policing we see an increased blurring between the two. Where the former aligns with the democratic ideals of the separation of powers and due process, driven by the logic of evidence and concrete cases, one of the defining aspects of high policing is the 'conflation of legal, judicial and executive power' (Brodeur, 2007, p. 32), accompanied by the insatiable hunger for intelligence and data. Anti-policies that stimulate the growth of privatized intelligence and high policing tend to delegate these latter forms of unaccountability to corporations as well as public institutions; the employer is both justified to collect intelligence and monitor staff, clients, students, and others, while also feeling entitled to act as police, prosecutor, and judge in one, such as in the cases of internal and workplace investigations (Kuldova & Nordrik, forthcoming; Nordrik & Kuldova, 2021). In the next part of this essay, we will discuss these forms of unaccountability and injustice (even when sold through the language of audit, accounting, and bureaucratic procedural justice). For now, let it suffice to say that these are legitimized precisely in much the same way as high policing and intelligence itself. This is not surprising as they result from the very legal obligations that enlist organizations in the fight against national security threats and global crime. We must remind ourselves here of the nature of symbolic legitimacy of high policing agencies, as Brodeur put it:

> Despite the fact that the police may, in reality, often break the law, it is not admissible to grant symbolic *legitimacy* to these violations because it would clash with the culture of trust binding police and citizens. The symbolic legitimacy of high policing agencies is the opposite: their lawlessness is the foundation of their mythology. The rogue culture fostered by fiction and by the media is that an intelligence agency is efficient in proportion to its disrespect of all rules; agents are even being blamed for being too fastidious in their respect for the law. However, this culture of institutionalized wrongdoing does not undermine the legitimacy of high policing for two reasons. First, it is covered either implicitly or explicitly by the authority of the state. (...). Second, it is justified on the (battle) ground that in order to defeat the enemy you may have to use same tactics. (Brodeur, 2007, p. 34)

While we may identify here a clear parallel between the mythology of corporate actors being celebrated in popular culture precisely for breaking the law, for finding smart loopholes, and for acting as the old rogues of the Gilded Age, what is more interesting is how this *sovereign* power of intelligence agencies—the power to break and transgress rules (Bataille, 1993), which normalizes the state of exception (Agamben, 1998)—has become delegated through anti-policies and paradoxically, compliance (!), to corporate and other actors. While some speak of the hollowing out of the state, of deregulation, as we have seen, the state is very much present and even hyper-active in issuing of new and ever more detailed regulation; some have assumed the state has surrendered its sovereignty, but it appears instead to be delegating it, expanding its reach and power rather than the reverse. The question is rather—whom it seeks to control and whom it delegates this sovereign power to. 'The state continues to have the ultimate authority over who may resort to coercion (...) the state structures the security network both in its presence and in its absence, both in its explicit directions and in its implicit permissions' (Loader & Walker, 2004, pp. 224–225) and it is the state that chooses to delegate this authority to corporations and, such as in the case countering radicalization, to public sector organizations, and thus in enlisting them—as we shall see in more detail later—through both legal and moral obligations, in the creation of a 'pre-crime society' (Arrigo & Sellers, 2021) and in the hyper-securitization and 'the creeping criminalization of everyday life' (Presdee, 2000, p. 159).

In practice, what is being delegated to these actors is the state authority to collect intelligence, to submit workers to surveillance, to internal investigations and interrogations, to punish and discipline, a delegation of authority legitimized by a fight against existential and extraordinary security threats—even if, in practice, translated into far less spectacular codes of conduct and ethics that, as we shall see, legitimize new forms of intelligence-led management and 'governance of the soul' of the workers (Rose, 1999). The crucial point is, however, that in building the architectures of compliance, one has paradoxically come to *strengthen* corporate sovereignty and stimulated the building of internal control, monitoring and surveillance systems that amount to nothing less than an architecture of a permanent technobureaucratic and managerial state of exception. In the process, the utilization of private intelligence in the service of corporate capital and in the name of the management and control of workers and others, and their recasting as possible offenders, insider threats, security risks, criminals, fraudsters, and so on, has been not only legitimized but even turned into the very essence of 'ethical business', 'corporate social responsibility', and 'stakeholder capitalism' with a human face. This may be read as the culmination of a long history of private policing, security, and intelligence serving capitalist expansion and the disciplining of labour; from Pinkerton's union busting via Ford's private army of ex-cops, ex-FBI agents, bouncers, and others to today's ex-intelligence officers in compliance and ethics departments, in consultancy and security firms, we see a historical continuity here (Weiss, 1986). Anti-policies create legal and moral *obligations* to monitor, surveil, gather intelligence, prevent, predict, pre-empt crime and security threats, and as such facilitate the growth of the compliance-industrial complex and the market for its products, normalize intelligence as a managerial logic, and most importantly, expand *corporate sovereignty*—the ability to break the law with impunity (Barkan, 2013), even in the name of the law. Again, here we should remind ourselves that in many jurisdictions the ability to prove the existence of an efficient compliance program, as well as voluntary disclosures and the like, result in lenient response from authorities. For instance, the DOJ's *FCPA Corporate Enforcement Policy*[15] states that,

> when a company has "voluntarily self-disclosed misconduct," "fully cooperated," and "timely and appropriately remediated," the DOJ may provide a "declination", by which it issues a letter voluntarily declining to prosecute. (...) In March 2018, Acting Attorney General John Cronan "announced that the Criminal Division would begin considering the *FCPA Corporate Enforcement Policy* as "nonbiding guidance" in *all* corporate criminal cases, not just those involving the FCPA. (Mamaysky, 2021, p. 69)

In practice, while there is a certain threat of enforcement actions, fines, reputational damage, even individual liability, building a compliance culture of ethics on top of a monitoring and auditing apparatus, can be interpreted as just another form of a *legally sanctioned immunity from the law*, thus redoubling the ways in which corporate sovereignty—as 'the paradoxical structure of power that emerges out of a complex of concrete practices that attempt to govern life by establishing and transgressing the boundaries of law' (Barkan, 2013, p. 7)—is expanded through compliance. Corporate sovereignty is thus expanded in two senses through the practices and enforcement of compliance: by expanding the intelligence capabilities of corporations as well as arenas where transgression

---

[15] https://www.justice.gov/criminal-fraud/file/838416/download (last accessed August 7, 2022).

of law becomes symbolically legitimate, and by creating opportunities for legally sanctioned immunity in a context of scandals, frauds, and public demands for *real* regulation of corporate abuse. Corporate sovereignty and expanded corporate power thus lurk behind the *simulations* of compliance and submission. It is precisely this willed politics of hybridization of policing and intelligence that institutes through the means of legal and moral obligation a pre-crime society and state of exception that forces us to recognize the role and increasing power of compliance, audit, and RegTech industries in prevention and enforcement of securitized global criminal law.

Why Bother About the Compliance-Industrial Complex?

While it is near impossible to argue against anti-policies directed at combatting different forms of global evils—after all, who can be for corruption—we need to turn our critical gaze at the ways in which we have chosen to actually go about combatting these evils. As we have seen, in practice this is done through the development of bureaucratic and managerial control systems that rely on the logic of accounting (Ala & Lapsley, 2019). These systems also rely on increasingly granular data and predictive software built around particular conceptions of risk, threat, and crime; these tools in turn rely on risk profiling and methods imported from intelligence and intelligence-led and (predictive) policing (Fyfe et al., 2018). Background checks, behavioural profiling, and risk prediction of employees, clients, suppliers, or third parties, insider threat management systems, open-source intelligence (OSINT) for the purposes of KYC, enhanced due diligence or sanctions screening, as well as private investigations, are just a few examples of technologies and intelligence logics incorporated into compliance management systems.

The compliance-industrial complex is, as we have seen, a transversal phenomenon. It is positioned at the intersection of the anti-corruption industry (Sampson, 2012), the anti-money laundering complex (Verhage, 2011), the private intelligence industry (Keefe, 2010), the private security industry and corporate security (Fitzgibbon & Lea, 2020; Schreier & Caparini, 2005; Walby & Lippert, 2014), human or rather inhuman resource management (Steyaert & Janssens, 1999), RegTech and FinTech with their products powered by artificial intelligence, data analytics and psychometrics (Barberis et al., 2019; Romero & Fitz, 2021), and the audit and accountancy industry with its army of lawyers, auditors, and consultants and key players such as the Big Four (Deloitte, Ernst & Young, KPMG, PwC), often treading an increasingly fine line between entrepreneurship and fraud (Shore & Wright, 2018; Sikka, 2016); this is not to mention the armies of lobbyists, NGOs, and other players involved in the making, shaping, and spreading of anti-policies. The compliance-industrial complex is more than the sum of its parts; it disregards the artificial disciplinary and legal subject matter boundaries and instead works towards integrating disparate legal, cultural, and ethical compliance subjects into the same platforms. It mirrors both the anti-policies and, in the industry lingo, it breaks down the silos; as such, it can be seen as the next level of what has been described as the striving towards 'security convergence' in 'governance through corporate security' (Wakefield, 2014, p. 236). It is precisely this *more* that remains unaddressed as research focuses narrowly on its multiple constitutive parts, details, and particulars. In the daily emails I receive from across a range of compliance providers and media outlets, I am bombarded with messaging that promotes breaking down of silos, and holistic and integrated approaches: 'how can I break down silos while fulfilling my regulatory obligations?', 'recognize and identify the silos to change the mindset', 'break down silos, and question the status quo', 'with regulatory requirements and penalties on the rise, forward-thinking firms are turning to holistic conduct surveillance to reduce conduct risk', 'Request a demo - SURVEIL-X Holistic Conduct Surveillance', 'thank you for downloading our eBook | A Guide To Holistic Third-Party Risk Assessment', 'A Holistic View of Risk with Connected Intelligence | Register today!', 'Centralising multiple GRC programs into one integrated platform', and so on.

As a transversal phenomenon par excellence, compliance as governance and as a form of policing has received scarce attention in critical criminology, legal anthropology, and critical management studies. While many have addressed particular aspects of this complex in one way or another, there have been few attempts to make sense of the complex realities that do not neatly submit to disciplinary and thematic boundaries. We have therefore few accounts that explicitly address the hybridization, securitization, and criminalization of compliance, governance, regulation, and managerial control in the context of 'surveillance capitalism' (Zuboff, 2019), where data as the new oil fuels the expansion of intrusive security products. This essay is a modest attempt to pull these threads together. The role of the compliance industry in global crime and security governance has similarly been often neglected by critical scholars, indeed with few significant exceptions (e.g. Haugh, 2017; Liss & Sharman, 2015; Nelson, 2021; Sampson, 2021; Tsingou, 2018; Verhage, 2011). Academic publications on compliance tend to focus on legal frameworks, risk management, and more pragmatic issues of corporate governance (e.g. Jackman, 2015; Manacorda & Cetonze, 2022; McBarnet, 2001; Nelson, 2021). Governmental and multilateral bodies involved in financial crime governance are indeed receiving increased attention—such as the Financial Action Task Force (FATF), G7, and other makers of the global AML and anti-corruption policy, and of the AML/CFT transnational legal order as such (de Oliveira, 2018; Halliday et al., 2019; Nance, 2018; Tilahun, 2021; Young & Woodiwiss, 2021). However, works focusing on institutions and regulators often tend to ignore or underplay the *hybrid* regulatory formations in which the compliance industry inserts itself and which allow it to grow beyond itself, so to speak—at the same time as they tend to gloss over the hegemonic power of the compliance-industrial complex as such. Institutionalist and political science perspectives dominate at the expense of more critical approaches. Insights from critical management studies (Alvesson & Willmott, 2003) which could facilitate the understanding of how regulatory agendas translate into concrete *management* solutions have also been largely ignored.

If we do not bring insights from critical management studies into criminology, we may possibly fail to grasp the reach of these proliferating architectures of internal policing and the social consequences of the 'criminalization of compliance' (Haugh, 2017). Private sector interest organizations, private standard setting and non-profit organizations, multinational corporations, global audit companies, and other private international organizations that churn out endless guidelines, voluntary codes, and best practice standards or translate these into products and software have become increasingly important private transnational regulators (Cafaggi, 2010) and players shaping global crime governance. The paradox is that the more criminalized compliance management systems become, at least vis-à-vis those they are designed to control—be it employees, clients, customers, or suppliers—the more we see the proliferation of 'playful' regulatory sandboxes at the top, where regulators become creative sparring partners who jointly 'explore' regulation in the name of innovation rather than acting as 'police' vis-à-vis the regulated entities. In this sense, structural inequalities and relations of privilege appear to be reproduced in the very regulatory set-up. Overall, we see private sector actors 'entering the international AML/CTF policy-making sphere' and 'significantly influencing global governance and challenging the primacy of the state' (de Oliveira, 2018, p. 154), and increasingly shaping the very regulation they are to submit to.

The COVID-19 pandemic and the, at the time of writing, ongoing war in Ukraine have further expanded the markets for RegTech and stimulated the technosolutionist appetites of governments and the modus operandi of risk-based near-real-time governance by numbers (Kuldova, 2022). COVID-19 policies have pushed many into remote work, accelerating datafication and simultaneously generating new threat scenarios: from cybersecurity to new internal and external threats, risks, and fraudulent schemes. The market for worker surveillance and digital defence architectures against a broad spectre of crimes, frauds, and security threats boomed. The war in Ukraine and the extraordinary expansion of sanctions regimes have, too, stimulated markets for data-driven sanctions screening tools, financial and other intelligence products, and profiling services for enhanced due diligence, third-party screening, and more. Tools, such as World-Check, formerly owned by Thompson Reuters, now owned by Refinitiv,[16] suddenly emerged out of their obscurity, at least partially. The recent class action against Thompson Reuters CLEAR Investigation Software[17] has also placed the industry on the radar of civil rights organizations. The class action offers a sneak peek into how Thompson Reuters goes about scraping personal data, turning these into a product that 'aggregates public and non-public information to create detailed cradle-to-grave dossiers on each person, including names, photographs, criminal history, relatives, associates, financial information, and employment information'[18] and assigns risk scores to individuals and delivers this information to anyone willing to pay, with often profound consequences and with no real possibility to challenge these opaque decisions

---

[16] https://www.refinitiv.com/en/products/world-check-kyc-screening (last accessed May 5, 2022).

[17] https://legal.thomsonreuters.com/en/products/clear-investigation-software (last accessed May 5, 2022).

[18] https://static1.squarespace.com/static/5c1bfc7eee175995a4ceb638/t/611ab5b00 0e2ae1d9bea3544/1629142044750/2021-0816+%28%2353%29+cand+ORDER+by+ Judge+Edward+M.+Chen+Granting+in+Part+and+Denying+in+Part+28+Defendants+Mot ion+to+Dismis.pdf (last accessed April 4, 2022).

and without any easy way to opt-out (an opt-out in fact requires finding a tiny link on the website and uploading official ID and real-time photo, thus harvesting even more sensitive private data). Like many similar products, this software is sold as an investigative tool for the purposes of compliance—be it AML, KYC, enhanced due diligence or CTF, for the needs of law enforcement agencies and even for investigations of healthcare fraud.[19] Refinitiv similarly provides an extremely broad range of compliance solutions and 'risk intelligence'[20] in the name of fighting fraud, crimes, corruption, and whatever comes to be deemed a security threat. And so does Palantir with its products such as Foundry, a company which has become notorious for its predictive policing technologies.[21] The consequences of a world shaped in the image of criminalized and securitized compliance will be manifold, but we may risk becoming so subjectivized by these hybrid governance architectures that we may no longer even notice.

At the same time, not only crimes, but also minor breaches become perceived through the lens of crime and treated *as if* they were crime and/or security threats. This development has been stimulated by both regulators and a market selling ever new tools for technobureaucratic control, tools to be employed in the name of the 'good' (Arrigo & Sellers, 2021; Hansen, 2018; McCulloch & Wilson, 2016) and zero tolerance policies—be it against corruption, harassment, or bullying. This market relies on the 'extension of public authority into the corporate sector' (Hansen, 2018) and on the extension of the power of the criminal justice system into organizations across both private and public sector, thus also extending the reach of criminal sanctions (Freeley, 2016; Lageson, 2020). 'Criminalized compliance' (Haugh, 2017) becomes further entrenched as a particular mode of control of deviance, increasingly managed through algorithmic architectures and data-driven technologies supplied by the RegTech industry and compliance platform providers. These compliance control infrastructures stretch all the way from the criminal in legal terms to the moral and ethical: from spectacular fraud, corruption, financial

---

[19] https://legal.thomsonreuters.com/en/products/clear-investigation-software   (last accessed April 4, 2022).

[20] https://www.refinitiv.com/en/risk-and-compliance# (last accessed April 4, 2022).

[21] https://www.palantir.com/assets/xrfr7uokpv1b/30qJLVSKsB5ZmfsvOydob6/a8e 340705b1e71ef325d1839fb97ce6f/Foundry_AMLpdf.pdf (last accessed August 10, 2022).

crimes, terrorism financing, cybercrime, organized crime, money laundering, and sexual harassment to minor breaches of etiquette, ethical codes, and 'micro-aggressions' of employees. Irrespective of their magnitude or seriousness, in these platforms they are lined up next to each other—all to be handled through the same risk scoring technologies, insider threat management systems, monitoring and surveillance platforms, scorecards, benchmarks, case management systems, and 'culture assessments tools'—and integrated into the same platform, differences, and complex realities flattened out, reduced to indicators, and handled through standardized systems. The result is a combination of 'greedy' and 'total institutions' (Coser, 1974; Goffman, 1968) that demand undivided commitment, submission, and obedience, while controlling conduct and any indications of transgression at ever more granular level.

Despite these efforts to control and govern through increasingly complex compliance and technobureaucratic structures, through auditing, reporting, 'holistic' risk management techniques (Wakefield, 2014), indicators, statistics, programming, and engineering of the social, corporate crimes and the facilitation of crime by corporates does not appear to be affected in any serious way. To the contrary, one could even argue that criminalized compliance is criminogenic, and that the frenetic attempts to control (mis)conduct and to overlay the societal moral vacuum and confusion with formalized, quantifiable, and internally prosecutable 'ethical culture' is merely accelerating social disintegration and anomie (Durkheim, 1947). The attempts to control corruption, as crime, as a security threat, and as a form of immoral conduct and general moral decay, are symptomatic—they are not accidentally at the core of the compliance-industrial complex. The compliance-industrial complex, and its mode of governance *by* numbers (Supiot, 2017) and *as* securitized and criminalized compliance, raises profound questions of the nature of the transformation of social control under neoliberalism and the devolution of rights, liberties, and justice that this form of governance appears to accelerate. The compliance-industrial complex is instrumental in the shaping of a 'pre-crime society' (Arrigo & Sellers, 2021). The role of compliance is often unrecognized, but once we understand it, it becomes clear that we must go beyond the criminal justice system and beyond the security- and military-industrial complexes to comprehend the progressive criminalization and securitization of society. Compliance is instrumental in the naturalization of a pre-crime society, a society that can be described, with Arrigo, Sellers, and Butta, as follows:

When privacy disappears as we know it, when coexistence is mediated by dataveillance regimes of human extension and abstraction, and when subjectivity is endlessly transformed into algorithmic profiles, then the society of pre-crime prevails. This is the destabilizing condition of ultra-modern age. In this society, the activities of risk-avoidance and threat analysis represent governing modes of human relating. Technology is pivotal to normalizing and nurturing this crime control enterprise. (…) The creeping criminalization of everyday life is guaranteed, and correspondingly, new and disturbing forms of people-making (i.e. of human relating) abound. (Arrigo et al., 2021, p. 11)

In the next part of this book, we shall look at the knowledge-power nexus that sustains the compliance-industrial complex and the ways in which it is fashioning a pre-crime society.

REFERENCES

Agamben, G. (1998). *Homo Sacer: Sovereign power and bare life*. Stanford University Press.

Ala, A. S., & Lapsley, I. (2019, 2019/09/01/). Accounting for crime in the neoliberal world. *The British Accounting Review, 51*(5). https://doi.org/10.1016/j.bar.2019.100839

Althusser, L. (1971). Ideology and ideological state apparatuses. In T. B. Brewster (Ed.), *Lenin and philosophy, and other essays* (pp. 127–188). New Left Books.

Alvesson, M., & Willmott, H. (Eds.). (2003). *Studying management critically*. Sage.

Arrigo, B., & Sellers, B. (Eds.). (2021). *The pre-crime society: Crime, culture and control in the ultramodern age*. Bristol University Press. https://doi.org/10.1332/policypress/9781529205251.001.0001

Arrigo, B., Sellers, B., & Butta, F. (2021). Introduction: The ultramodern age of criminology, control societies and 'dividual' justice policy. In B. Arrigo & B. Sellers (Eds.), *The pre-crime society: Crime, culture and control in the ultramodern age* (pp. 1–14). Bristol University Press. https://doi.org/10.1332/policypress/9781529205251.003.0001

Barberis, J., Arner, D. W., & Buckley, R. P. (2019). *The RegTech book: The financial technology handbook for investors, entrepreneurs and visionaries in regulation*. Willey.

Barkan, J. (2013). *Corporate sovereignty: Law and government under capitalism*. University of Minnesota Press. https://doi.org/10.5749/minnesota/9780816674268.001.0001

Bataille, G. (1993). *The accursed share: Volumes II and III*. Zone Books.

Baudrillard, J. (1994). *Simulacra and simulation*. University of Michigan Press. https://doi.org/10.3998/mpub.9904

Brodeur, J.-P. (2007). High and low policing in post-9/11 times. *Policing, 1*(1), 25–37. https://doi.org/10.1093/police/pam002

Cafaggi, F. (2010). *New foundations of transnational private regulation*. https://doi.org/10.2139/ssrn.1953925

Coser, L. A. (1974). *Greedy institutions: Patterns of undivided commitment*. The Free Press.

de Oliveira, I. S. (2018). The governance of the financial action task force: An analysis of power and influence throughout the years. *Crime, Law and Social Change, 69*, 153–172. https://doi.org/10.1007/s10611-017-9749-4

Durkheim, E. (1947). *The division of labor in society*. The Free Press.

Fitzgibbon, W., & Lea, J. (2020). *Privatising justice: The security industry, war and crime control*. Pluto Press. https://doi.org/10.2307/j.ctvzsmdsj

Freeley, M. M. (2016). Entrepreneurs of punishment: How private contractors made and are making the modern criminal justice system—An account of convict transportation and electronic monitoring. *Justice, Law & Society, 17*(3), 1–30.

Fyfe, N., Gundhus, H., & Rønn, K. V. (Eds.). (2018). *Moral issues in intelligence-led policing*. Routledge. https://doi.org/10.4324/9781315231259

Garrett, B. L. (2014). *Too big to jail: How prosecutors compromise with corporations*. The Belknap Press of Harvard University Press. https://doi.org/10.4159/9780674735712

Goffman, E. (1968). *Asylums: Essays on the social situation of mental patients and other inmates*. Penguin.

Halliday, T., Levi, M., & Reuter, P. (2019). Anti-money laundering: An inquiry into a disciplinary transnational legal order. *UCI Journal of International, Transnational, and Comparative Law, 4*(1–25).

Hansen, H. K. (2018). Policing corruption post- and pre-crime: Collective action and private authority in maritime industry. *Indiana Journal of Global Legal Studies, 25*(1), 131–156. https://doi.org/10.2979/indjglolegstu.25.1.0131

Haugh, T. (2017). The criminalization of compliance. *Notre Dame Law Review, 92*(3), 1215–1270.

Hayes, B. (2012). The surveillance-industrial complex. In K. Ball, K. D. Haggerty, & D. Lyon (Eds.), *Routledge handbook of surveillance studies* (pp. 167–175). Routledge. https://doi.org/10.4324/9780203814949.ch2_2_c

Hunt, A. (1999). *Governing morals: A social history of moral regulation*. Cambridge University Press.

Jackman, D. (2015). *The compliance revolution: How compliance needs to change to survive*. Wiley. https://doi.org/10.1002/9781119045922

Keefe, P. R. (2010). Privatized spying: The emerging intelligence industry. In L. K. Johnson (Ed.), *The Oxford handbook of national security intelligence* (pp. 297–310). Oxford University Press. https://doi.org/10.1093/oxfordhb/9780195375886.003.0018

Kuldova, T. Ø. (2022). Thinking the delirious pandemic governance by numbers with Samit Basu's chosen spirits and Prayaag Akbar's Leila. *Journal of Postcolonial Writing*, 1–16. https://doi.org/10.1080/17449855.2022.2040801

Kuldova, T. Ø., & Nordrik, B. (forthcoming). Workplace investigations and the hollowing out of the Norwegian model of co-determination. *Class and Capital*.

Lageson, S. E. (2020). *Digital punishment: Privacy, stigma, and the harms of data-driven criminal justice*. Oxford University Press. https://doi.org/10.1093/oso/9780190872007.001.0001

Levi-Faur, D. (2017). Regulatory capitalism. In P. Drahos (Ed.), *Regulatory theory: Foundation and applications* (pp. 289–302). ANU Press. https://doi.org/10.22459/RT.02.2017.17

Liss, C., & Sharman, J. C. (2015). Global corporate crime-fighters: Private transnational responses to piracy and money laundering. *Review of International Political Economy, 22*(4), 693–718. https://doi.org/10.1080/09692290.2014.936482

Loader, I. (2000). Plural policing and democratic governance. *Social & Legal Studies, 9*(3), 323–345. https://doi.org/10.1177/096466390000900301

Loader, I., & Walker, N. (2004). State of denial? Rethinking the governance of security. *Punishment and Society, 6*(2), 221–228. https://doi.org/10.1177/1462474504041267

Lobel, O. (2012). New governance as regulatory governance. In D. Levi-Faur (Ed.), *The Oxford handbook of governance* (pp. 65–82). Oxford University Press. https://doi.org/10.1093/oxfordhb/9780199560530.013.0005

Mamaysky, I. (2021). Understanding ethics and compliance: A practitioner's guide to effective corporate compliance programs. *Journal of Regulatory Compliance* (VI), 58–108. https://doi.org/10.2139/ssrn.3789983

Manacorda, S., & Cetonze, F. (Eds.). (2022). *Corporate compliance on a global scale: Legitimacy and effectiveness*. Springer. https://doi.org/10.1007/978-3-030-81655-1

McBarnet, D. (2001). *When compliance is not the solution but the problem: From changes in the law to changes in attitude*. (Working Paper No. 18). Australian National University, Centre for Tax System Integrity.

McCulloch, J., & Wilson, D. (2016). *Pre-crime: Pre-emption, precaution and the future*. Routledge. https://doi.org/10.4324/9781315769714

Nance, M. T. (2018). The regime that FATF built: An introduction to Financial Action Task Force. *Crime, Law and Social Change, 69*, 109–129. https://doi.org/10.1007/s10611-017-9747-6

Nelson, J. S. (2021). Compliance as management. In B. V. Rooij & D. D. Sokol (Eds.), *The Cambridge handbook of compliance* (pp. 104–122). Cambridge University Press. https://doi.org/10.1017/9781108759458.009

Nordrik, B., & Kuldova, T. Ø. (2021). *Faktaundersøkelser - et "hybrid konflik-tvåpen" på norske arbeidsplasser.* Gyldendal Akademisk.

O'Hara, S. P. (2016). *Inventing the Pinkertons or spies, sleuths, mercenaries, and thugs.* John Hopkins University Press.

Presdee, M. (2000). *Cultural criminology and the carnival of crime.* Routledge.

Roland, A. (2007). The military-industrial complex: Lobby and trope. In A. J. Bacevich (Ed.), *The long war: A new history of U.S. national security policy since World War II* (pp. 355–370). Columbia University Press.

Romero, P., & Fitz, S. (2021). The use of psychometrics and artificial intelligence in alternative finance. In R. Rau, R. Wardrop, & L. Zingales (Eds.), *The Palgrave handbook of technological finance* (pp. 511–587). Palgrave. https://doi.org/10.1007/978-3-030-65117-6_21

Rose, N. (1999). *Governing the soul: The shaping of the private self.* Free Association Books.

Sampson, S. (2012). The anti-corruption industry: From movement to institution. In D. Schmidt-Pfister & H. Moroff (Eds.), *Fighting corruption in Eastern Europe: A multilevel perspective.* Routledge.

Sampson, S. (2021). Good people doing bad things: Compliance regimes in organisations. *Journal of Legal Anthropology, 5*(1), 110–134. https://doi.org/10.3167/jla.2021.050105

Schreier, F., & Caparini, M. (2005). *Privatising security: Law, practice and governance of private military and security companies.* Geneva Centre for the Democratic Control of Armed Forces (DCAF) Occasional Paper No. 6.

Shore, C., & Wright, S. (2018). How the Big 4 got big: Audit culture and the metamorphosis of international accountancy firms. *Critique of Anthropology, 38*(3), 303–324. https://doi.org/10.1177/0308275X18775815

Sikka, P. (2016). Big four accounting firms: Addicted to tax avoidance. In J. Haslam & P. Sikka (Eds.), *Pioneers of critical accounting: A celebration of the life of Tony Lowe* (pp. 259–274). Palgrave Macmillan. https://doi.org/10.1057/978-1-137-54212-0_13

Steyaert, C., & Janssens, M. (1999). Human and inhuman resource management: Saving the subject of HRM. *Organization, 6*(2), 181–198. https://doi.org/10.1177/135050849962002

Supiot, A. (2017). *Governance by numbers: The making of a legal model of allegiance.* Bloomsbury.

Taylor, H. (2006). *The Joy of SOX: Why Sarbanes-Oxley and service-oriented architecture may be the best thing that ever happened to you.* Wiley.

Tilahun, N. (2021). The re-organization of the FATF as an international legal person and the promises and limits to accountability. In A. Arcuri & F. Coman-Kund (Eds.), *Technocracy and the law: Accountability, governance and expertise* (pp. 131–154). Routledge. https://doi.org/10.4324/978100317 4769-6

Tsingou, E. (2018). New governors on the block: The rise of anti-money laundering professionals. *Crime, Law and Social Change, 69,* 191–205. https://doi.org/10.1007/s10611-017-9751-x

Veggeland, N. (2009). *Taming the regulatory state: Politics and ethics.* Edward Elgar.

Veggeland, N. (2010). *Den nye reguleringsstaten: Idébrytinger og styringskonflikter.* Gyldendal Akademisk.

Verhage, A. (2011). *The anti money laundering complex and the compliance industry.* Routledge. https://doi.org/10.4324/9780203828489

Wakefield, A. (2014). Corporate security and enterprise risk management. In K. Walby & R. K. Lippert (Eds.), *Corporate security in the 21st century: Theory and practice in international perspective.* Palgrave Macmillan. https://doi.org/10.1057/9781137346070_13

Walby, K., & Lippert, R. K. (2014). *Corporate security in the 21st century: Theory and practice in international perspective.* Palgrave Macmillan. https://doi.org/10.1057/9781137346070

Weiss, R. P. (1986). Private detective agencies and labour discipline in the United States, 1855–1946. *The Historical Journal, 29*(1), 87–101. https://doi.org/10.1017/S0018246X0001863X

Weiss, R. P. (2008). From cowboy detectives to soldiers of fortune: Private security contracting and its contradictions on the new frontier of capitalist expansion. *Social Justice, 34*(3/4), 1–19.

Ylönen, M., & Kuusela, H. (2019). Consultocracy and its discontents: A critical typology and a call for a research agenda. *Governance, 32,* 241–258. https://doi.org/10.1111/gove.12369

Young, M. A., & Woodiwiss, M. (2021). A world fit for money laundering: The Atlantic alliance's undermining of organized crime control. *Trends in Organized Crime, 24,* 70–95. https://doi.org/10.1007/s12117-020-093 86-8

Zedner, L. (2007). Pre-crime and post-criminology? *Theoretical Criminology, 11*(2), 261–281. https://doi.org/10.1007/s12117-020-09386-8

Zuboff, S. (2019). *The age of surveillance capitalism: The fight for a human future at the new frontier of power.* Profile Books.

PART II

Compliance as the Operating System of a Pre-Crime Society

Introduction to Part II: Compliance as the Operating System of a Pre-Crime Society

Abstract In this brief chapter, we introduce Part II of this book and (re)focus on how the *preventive* state has delegated its authority and extraordinary powers to corporations, regulated businesses, and other organizations. Or else, on how it has outsourced its powers to manufacture suspicion to a broad range of organizations, actors, and individuals who cast themselves as crime fighters. We consider how the state has thus empowered and legitimized internal managerial apparatuses, and their pre-emptive security and risk management practices—not only compliance, but also human resource management and in-house corporate security departments. None of this would be possible without the experts and professionals that shape the 'legalization' of organizational governance; this expertise is then built into the algorithmic architectures and managerial systems.

Keywords Legalization · Preventive state · Post-politicization · Expertise · Technobureaucracy

Anti-policies have not only created new markets for the compliance-industrial complex but also enhanced corporate sovereignty, rather than undermining it. State authority has been delegated to corporations, regulated business, and other organizations, now enlisted in the fight against

T. Ø. Kuldova, *Compliance-Industrial Complex*, https://doi.org/10.1007/978-3-031-19224-1_4

crime, corruption, and security threats. Their *internal* managerial apparatus, their compliance departments, their IT infrastructures, their HR
departments, and last but not least, their *in-house* security departments
have been mobilized in the pursuit of foreign policy agendas and crime
fighting alike. While all can agree that it is important to fight these
crimes, that stopping fraud and uncovering suspicious transactions that
can point the financial crime units to organized crime, drug trade, human
trafficking, weapons, and more and that banks and financial institutions
but also other organizations should reasonably protect their clients from
fraud, there is a potential dark side to the manufacturing of suspicion
when it becomes a *default* setting. There is also a dark side to the
outsourcing of the power to manufacture suspicion, to *define what is
deemed suspicious* and what not and even to act on it, to powerful
corporate actors.

The delegation or acquisition of this power has not been in any
way a straightforward process. Imagining it as such would be to miss
the networked and hybrid forms of contemporary governance discussed
earlier (Solomon, 2010). It is not always easy to distinguish between
voluntary industry self-regulation and standard setting which often
attempts to pre-empt state regulation as well as public pressure and state
regulation as such—not less because these often converge, such as in
the case of supervised self-regulation (O'Connor et al., 2008). It would
also be to miss the industries' desire and lobbying for regulation and for
being regulated—precisely in order to be seen as *legitimate* actors (White,
2014), such as in the case of the private security industry. This, after all,
allows the industry actors to market themselves also as 'state-deputized
institutions functioning in accordance with the state-guaranteed public
good' (White, 2014, p. 44). During compliance and anti-corruption
conferences which I have attended, and where the representatives of
the state and financial intelligence units were present, it became abundantly clear to me that the demand for more regulation came from the
compliance industry professionals, often despite the rather reluctant position of the representatives of the state authorities. Regulation translates
into markets for the industry, into demand for a particular increasingly
specialized but simultaneously also increasingly comprehensive compliance expertise, but it also *legitimizes* the internal corporate security and
managerial apparatus.

In most jurisdictions, corporate in-house security has been largely unregulated and invisible in public debate, overshadowed by the discussions about private security actors, and the more obvious forms of contractualization and outsourcing of police and state powers (White, 2014). But the in-house security and compliance apparatuses have clearly not been invisible to the states, who have become ready to both 'govern *through*' them and delegate their authority and power to them (O'Connor et al., 2008). But in what sense precisely? Criminologists and legal scholars have been debating the growth and reshaping of the 'preventive state', which has fostered 'new practices of preventive criminalization, policing and punishment', motivated by 'the preventive impetus to minimize risks and forestall harms' (Zedner & Ashworth, 2019, pp. 429–430). What is being delegated are the authority and extraordinary powers of such a *preventive* state, which both aligns with and legitimizes pre-existing pre-emptive security and risk management practices, such as those of in-house corporate security, while incorporating these into the state 'regulatory toolbox' via compliance.

In an era that fetishizes the *expert*, in both private and public governance, and where many of these experts operate across jurisdictions, and where the ambition is nothing less than 'universal' standards and best practices, it becomes even more difficult to draw any clear distinctions between the private and the public. With the experts who themselves regularly cross these imaginary boundaries, the expert knowledge also travels and translates internationally from one location to another (Wedel, 2014). Legal and compliance, but increasingly also risk and security, management and HR personnel professionals 'filter' regulations and soft and hard law alike, as they market their services, seek professional legitimacy, and place within organizations: 'they construct not only the meaning of law but also the magnitude of the threat posed by law and the litigiousness of the legal environment' (Edelman et al., 1992, p. 49). These professionals, globally networked, are important drivers in the diffusion of organizational practices and in the translation and interpretation of legal texts, and in the dissemination of this expert knowledge, thus both shaping the meanings of and co-constructing law. Relying on these accredited, certified, and trained experts, the 'employer's understanding of the law may be the result of several layers of filters, each of which has the potential to embellish or alter its meaning and implications' (Edelman et al., 1992, p. 49). And hence while in one jurisdiction a certain procedure may be a matter of legal compliance, in another jurisdiction the same may be implemented in a pre-emptive and aspirational fashion, while organizations across these jurisdictions may have very different levels of both understanding and implementation, depending on their size and nature. Despite this, standards produced by 'technical' experts are often deemed universal. Or as ISO management system standards remind us, these are 'applicable to all types of organizations regardless of the type, size and nature of the activity, as well as whether the organization is from the public, private or non-profit sector'.[1]

What is often missed in the state-centric literature on regulation is precisely the role of these experts and of the compliance-industrial complex in manufacturing voluntary self-regulation, in the translation and appropriation of laws and so on, in their repackaging into products, from trainings, certifications, guides and reports, consulting, auditing, to software and more that are precisely intended to cross jurisdictions and be treated *as if* universal standards. What we are thus dealing with is the layering of governance, both through governance itself and through expert knowledge production, or as Bartley puts it:

> These standards have proliferated rapidly since the 1990s, in the form of voluntary policies and codes of conduct adopted by individual companies, collective standards adopted by groups of companies, and third-party systems for certifying compliance. (…) Contrary to much of the discourse surrounding them, these standards do not simply add new rules for previously ungoverned phenomena. Rather, they add an additional layer of rules for phenomena that are already embedded in complex political, legal, and regulatory orders. (…) Yet the growing literature on social and environmental standards, codes of conduct, and certification systems routinely ignores this layering of rules, instead portraying private standards as filling a 'regulatory void' or 'governance gap' created by the inability or unwillingness of states and international bodies to regulate a world of mobile capital and global supply chains. (Bartley, 2011, pp. 518–519)

It is precisely this layering that further contributes to the regulatory hybridization and blurring, as anti-policies become translated into expert products, private standards, into codes of conduct and ethics, into voluntary guidance. In practice, this often amounts to layers of (self-)regulatory

---

[1] Here using the example of ISO 37301:2021 compliance management systems— Requirements with guidance for use https://www.iso.org/obp/ui/fr/#iso:std:iso:37301: ed-1:v1:en (last accessed August 17, 2022).

self-protection, of layering of plausible deniability, of delegations of responsibility and accountability. Or as Bartley puts it: 'firms initially developed codes of conduct to shield themselves from several types of external pressures. In at least some instances, they then used their engagement in voluntary efforts as a way to ward off further government intervention' (Bartley, 2005, p. 227). This layering is accompanied and also made possible by increasing 'legalization' of organizational governance, which has turned the large corporate and bureaucratic organization into an 'entire private legal system in its own right' (Edelman & Suchman, 1999), resulting in the *imitation* and hybridization of the legal order as organizations have internalized law-like rulemaking. As Edelman and Suchman observe in their brilliant piece on this transformation, *When the 'Haves' Hold Court,*

> By merging roles of legislator, administrator, forum, judge, lawyer, and cop, such organizations have colonized the base of the disputing pyramid and have infused it with a distinctly managerial logic. As this colonization has proceeded, the new private legal order has annexed increasingly large segments of territory from the traditional public legal order, subtly shifting the balance between democratic and bureaucratic tendencies in society (Edelman & Suchman, 1999, p. 985). (...) It is the merging of these roles, however, that truly cements organizational power, both to regulate social behavior and to constitute social reality (cf. Edelman & Suchman, 1997). Although the consequences of legal internalization are often complex, and although internalization may involve considerable benefits for the 'have nots,' nonetheless when organizations hold court, the 'haves' tend to come out still further ahead (Edelman & Suchman, 1999, p. 976). (...) As private legislatures, courthouses, law offices, and police departments, organizations construct within and around themselves a semiautonomous legal regime that simultaneously mimics and absorbs even the most 'official' institutions of governmental law. (Edelman & Suchman, 1999, p. 943)

The compliance-industrial complex, its experts, and professionals have contributed to these processes of 'legalization' and hybridization, functioning as an apparatus, one that translates politics and law into techno-managerial dispositives, thus narrowing down the political domain, while subjectivizing its proponents and cynics alike. This legalization, we should remind ourselves, can be also understood as 'a mechanism of bourgeois hegemony, a device for obscuring capitalist control by shifting the locus of power from direct coercion to impersonal, universalistic rules'

(Edelman & Suchman, 1999, p. 947). Post-politicization follows. Swyngedouw has nicely described the process of 'post-politicization' or else 'the contested and uneven process by which consensual governance of contentious public affairs through the mobilization of techno-managerial dispositives sutures or colonizes the space of the political' and where 'technological, institutional, and managerial "fixes" are negotiated that leave the basic political-economic structure intact' (Swyngedouw, 2018, pp. xv–xvi). In this second part of the essay, we shall look more closely at the different forms of technobureaucratic expertise and knowledge as it commodifies itself and informs and shapes the products of the compliance-industrial complex. We will try to understand the power of this expertise, the way it perceives the world, and the way it tries to shape the world into its image, embedding its fantasies of control into the algorithmic architectures of compliance. Designing in the process an operating system of a pre-crime society, an infrastructure so naturalized, that it almost becomes imperceptible to the many. This is where the power of expertise as a form of 'extrastatecraft' materializes (Easterling, 2016). But before we delve into the realm of expertise and data, let us consider the role of the whistleblower, a case that most acutely reveals how such systems and noble visions quickly turn into their opposite, likely to police free speech, pre-empt critique, and supress dissent.

REFERENCES

Bartley, T. (2005). Corporate accountability and the privatization of labor standards: Struggles over codes of conduct in the apparel industry. *Research in Political Sociology*, 211–244. https://doi.org/10.1016/S0895-9935(05)140 07-8

Bartley, T. (2011). Transnational governance as the layering of rules: Intersections of public and private standards. *Theoretical Inquiries in Law, 12*(2), 517–542. https://doi.org/10.2202/1565-3404.1278

Easterling, K. (2016). *Extrastatecraft: The power of infrastructure space.* Verso.

Edelman, L. B., Abraham, S. E., & Erlanger, H. S. (1992). Professional construction of law: The inflated threat of wrongful discharge. *Law & Society Review, 26*(1), 47–84. https://doi.org/10.2307/3053836

Edelman, L. B., & Suchman, M. C. (1999). When the 'haves' hold court: Speculations on the organizational internalization of law. *Law & Society Review, 33*(4), 941–991. https://doi.org/10.2307/3115155

O'Connor, D., Lippert, R. K., Spencer, D., & Smylie, L. (2008). Seeing private security like a state. *Criminology & Criminal Justice, 8*(2), 203–226. https://doi.org/10.1177/1748895808088995

Solomon, J. M. (2010). New governance, preemptive self-regulation, and the blurring of boundaries in regulatory theory and practice. *Wisconsin Law Review*, 591–625.

Swyngedouw, E. (2018). *Promises of the political: Insurgent cities in a post-political environment.* MIT Press. https://doi.org/10.7551/mitpress/10668.001.0001

Wedel, J. (2014). *Unaccountable: How the establishment corrupted our finances.* Pegasus Books.

White, A. (2014). Beyond the regulatory gaze? corporate security, (in) visibility, and the modern state. In K. Walby & R. K. Lippert (Eds.), *Corporate security in the 21st century: Theory and practice in international perspective.* Palgrave Macmillan. https://doi.org/10.1057/9781137346070_3

Zedner, L., & Ashworth, A. (2019). The rise and restraint of the preventive state. *Annual Review of Criminology, 2*, 429–450. https://doi.org/10.1146/annurev-criminol-011518-024526

CHAPTER 5

The Pre-emption of Dissent

Abstract We turn to the case of whistleblowing, how whistleblowers are enlisted in the service of intelligence, anti-corruption, and more and to the systems set up to comply with whistleblowing regulation aimed at the protection of whistleblowers from retaliation and the systems designed to pre-empt dissent and prevent reputational damage. The (ambivalent) figure of the whistleblower, alternatively cast as a hero or an insider threat, often triggers the proactive intelligence-driven apparatus of in-house compliance and security. The algorithmic management systems that seek to control and even eliminate both internal and external threats *before* they materialize, and even to punish and sanction, thus come into the spotlight—as does the uncanny shift from whistleblower protection to insider threat management systems, both implemented in the name of compliance.

Keyword Whistleblowing · Insider threat management · Algorithmic management · Reputation · Risk · Human resource management

The complex apparatuses of power of the compliance-industrial complex become most visible when targeting or when trying to pre-empt critique, dissent, opposition, or simply, whatever is designated as non-compliance. In our previous research on workplace investigations, we have shown

© The Author(s), under exclusive license to Springer Nature Switzerland AG 2022
T. Ø. Kuldova, *Compliance-Industrial Complex*,
https://doi.org/10.1007/978-3-031-19224-1_5

precisely how an in-house or hired quasi-legal apparatus is mobilized in response to various complaints about mismanagement, managerial and performance pressures, professional disagreements, or reports on corruption. The complaint quickly triggered internal investigations that imitated police methods, the complainant, often without even knowing it, became labelled a 'whistleblower', forced to identify an individual or a small group the complaint was directed at, and legitimate critique, often pertaining to structural and organizational matters quickly became reframed as a matter of problematic individual(s), who were seen as displaying traits of 'counterproductive workplace behaviour', 'anti-social behaviour', or any other range of pop-psychological psychopathologies (Kenny et al., 2019)—especially when such a complaint involved senior management. A Kafkaesque investigation followed, a manifestation of the strategic weaponization of legalese, often resulting in grave psychological and financial harm to the one labelled as a 'whistleblower' (Kuldova & Nordrik, forthcoming; Nordrik & Kuldova, 2021), as well as to supportive colleagues and family who became collaterals. We came to the same conclusions as Edelman and Suchman (Edelman & Suchman, 1999), showing how internal investigations become *the* prime site where the organizational merger of the roles of legislator, judge, police officer, and prosecutor driven by a managerial logic, where both the hybrid practices and the pervasive sense of injustice thus induced become most acutely visible. Some of our informants deemed these apparatuses as causing grave injustice, undermining civil and human rights, eroding the freedom of speech, generating mistrust and fear cultures. We also showed how these investigations become a form of retaliation—even when conducted precisely within the framework of anti-retaliation policies supposed to guarantee whistleblower protection. But whistleblowers do not only trigger the *reactive investigative apparatus*, they are also increasingly seen as an 'insider threats', as a risk to be anticipated, monitored, and managed—as such they also trigger the *proactive intelligence-driven apparatus* of in-house compliance and security.

Whistleblowers were behind many of the corporate and governmental scandals and revelations. In the wake of these scandals, the cultural figure of the whistleblower emerged—as a heroic *individual* who often faces retaliation, sanctions, harassment, and threats and suffers great personal and financial harms, and 'symbolic extinction' (Kenny, 2019), only to reveal the truth of the system. Despite being often seen as a controversial figure, policy focus has been turned both to the role of whistleblowers as truth tellers doing public service, revealing corruption, fraud, and other harms and as those who need protection against retaliation (Ceva & Bocchiola, 2019). This hyper-focus on the individual, one often in an extremely weak position vis-à-vis powerful actors, chimes both with the logic of individual responsibilization and the imaginary of much of fraud as a matter of one or few 'bad apples', persistent in compliance as much as in much regulation, despite all the talk about culture. In 2022, Mary Lawlor, Special Rapporteur on the situation of human rights defenders for UN, published her short but influential report titled *At the heart of the struggle: human rights defenders working against corruption,*[1] arguing that protection frameworks applicable to human rights defenders should also apply to those who expose corrupt practices, while pointing to a range of threats and risks, including violence and murder, judicial harassment, intimidation, surveillance, smear campaigns, and other structural difficulties experienced by whistleblowers, activists, academics, lawyers, and other human rights defenders. This naturally contributes to elevating the status of those revealing corruption while further integrating anti-corruption into the human rights discourse, mirroring the increasing synergies between anti-policies. While it is again extremely important to protect those who speak out in public interest, all can agree on that, a paradox may emerge when the structures enforced in the name of protection risk ending up undermining these efforts, while at the same time empowering the corporate sovereign. This paradox is at the very heart of the trouble with compliance.

On the Enlisting of the Whistleblower in the Service of Intelligence

Whistleblowers are often perceived either as heroes or as traitors and snitches. They are ambivalent, morally ambiguous, transgressive, and 'abject' figures (Kristeva, 1982) as they break the unspoken rules of organizations with its codes of silence and loyalty (rather than breaking the declared compliance rules). They often end up positioned as deviant, ab-normal, non-compliant, difficult, and deranged. They become 'impossible beings' with 'impossible speech' (Kenny, 2019). They are either

---

[1] https://reliefweb.int/report/world/heart-struggle-human-rights-defenders-working-against-corruption-report-special (last accessed August 16, 2022).

celebrated for their ethical integrity within a corrupt system or against corrupt individuals, for their guts to speak out and serve the public, or they are cast as disloyal and thus to be penalized. Overall, researchers agree that 'the status quo is that whistleblowers will be retaliated against, they will suffer, and laws will continue to fail to protect them. This state of affairs continues, and it effectively institutionalizes the tragedy of the whistleblower' (Kenny, 2019, p. 30). Alas, whistleblowing came to be seen over the past decades as one of the most efficient ways to bring to light corrupt practices and fraud. The United States encourages whistleblowing through rewards and protections, through the False Claims Act (FCA) and the Dodd-Frank Act (2010). Whistleblowers can be financially rewarded provided the information leads to successful prosecution—such as in the notorious case of Bradley Birkenfeld (Birkenfeld, 2020), 'the first Swiss banker to successfully use the whistleblower program set up by the US Internal Revenue Service to expose and prosecute tax cheats'.[2] The US enlists *both* compliance departments and whistleblowers in its anticorruption and anti-fraud apparatus, while rewarding both—the former with lowered fines, the latter with financial rewards and not without resistance from capital owners: the Chamber of Commerce for instance 'lobbied lawmakers to amend the Dodd-Frank statute itself to impose the requirement of internal reporting' (Sylvia & Stabile, 2018, p. 455), or else, the requirement to run through internal compliance channels first, where the complaint (or its maker) can be contained and handled. The amendment was rejected, but there are so many codes of conduct and ethics associated with speak-up channels and so much compliance effort put into directing employees to the internal channels first that in practice raising voice internally is deemed 'best practice'. This indeed protects the organization, while the whistleblower, despite anti-retaliation policies, may face grave consequences or, alternatively, be ignored or provided a report that dismisses his or her allegations; this does not mean that in many instances these channels may function perfectly well, but it is impossible to get around the dramatic power imbalance and the individualization of responsibility (Gray, 2006). Much like in the area of workplace health and safety, where 'workers are being transformed from a victim to a

---

[2] https://www.whistleblower-rewards.eu/monetary-rewards (last accessed August 16, 2022). There is a considerable market for legal services, offering support to whistleblowers in order to reap the rewards, while doing good.

health and safety offender' (Gray, 2006, p. 875), even here we can discern the 'shift to regulation through individual responsibility', where

> workers are required to enforce regulation by policing their own hazards (through individual responsibility and the right to refuse) while, at the same time, increasingly becoming a target of regulation. This shift has resulted in a diffusion of responsibility over workplace safety risks and a blurring of responsibility between employers and employees over who is responsible for unsafe conditions found inside the workplace. Workers, when they do not refuse, are often then blamed for allowing the unsafe hazards to continue. (Gray, 2006, p. 888)

While there are academic discussions about whether whistleblowing should not only be a right, but also a duty (Ceva & Bocchiola, 2019), and whether it is reasonable or not to legislate such a duty (Vandekerckhove & Tsahuridu, 2010), in practice the *duty* of the employee or worker to report breaches of both law and internal codes can be written into contractual agreements or internal codes of ethics imposing such a duty on all employees, including the duty to report 'suspicion'.[3] The employee becomes individually responsible, both for the reporting of the suspicion and for the failure to do so; the duty to police each other and generate actionable intelligence for the management is enforceable under such codes (Sampson, 2019).

The EU, which likes to see itself as a global standard-setter in its regulatory efforts and likes to inspire with its regulatory models, has recently similarly recognized the usefulness of whistleblowers in providing intelligence on breaches of law, and also the need for the increased protection of whistleblowers. The *EU Whistleblower Directive* came into force on 17 December 2021, recognizing whistleblowers as instrumental in both information gathering and in deterrence, as whistleblowers 'can feed national and EU enforcement systems with information leading to effective detection, investigation and prosecution of breaches of Union rules'

---

[3] As an example, one can take for instance Alarmtech's Code of Conduct, clearly stating that 'It is your duty to report any suspected violations of the Code.' 'If you know of or suspect any potential human rights violations relating to our business, it is your duty to speak up' https://alarmtechglobal.com/img/code_of_conduct_EN.pdf or the Code of Conduct of Raiffeisen Informatic Group: 'If employees obtain knowledge of breaches against the Raiffeisen Informatik CoC, they must report the matter to their line manager or the Compliance division' https://www.ri-c.at/wp-content/uploads/2019/07/Code-of-Conduct-engl_13062016.pdf (last accessed August 19, 2022).

and as 'whistleblower protection can make it easier to detect, prevent and deter fraud, corruption and other illegal activities affecting the financial interests of the Union'.[4] The directive mandates all firms with more than 50 employees and all financial services providers irrespective of size, to establish internal whistleblowing channels (hence creating new market for the compliance-industrial complex). While the directive opens for external whistleblowing under certain specified conditions, it also states that 'if internal and external reporting channels are available, a whistleblower should use these first in order to be guaranteed protection under the new law' and only then, 'if the use of internal and/or external channels did not produce any results and the whistleblower did not receive appropriate feedback within the 3 or 6 month timeframe set by the new law, he/she can choose the last-resort option of publicly disclosing the information, for instance, directly to the public via web platforms or social media, or to the media, elected officials, civil society organisations etc'. It is also made clear that the law aims 'at protecting responsible whistleblowing, genuinely intended to safeguard the public interest, while proactively discouraging malicious whistleblowing and preventing unjustified reputational damage' and that 'Member States must also introduce effective, proportionate and dissuasive penalties for those who make malicious or abusive reports or disclosures'.[5] In other words, there is plenty of room to supress unwanted reports internally or to lead protracted legal battles over malicious intent, a well-documented corporate strategy of intimidation through legal blackmails (Glasbeek, 2002). Even in the law intended to protect whistleblowers, there is a fine line sketched in it between a hero and a 'malicious insider' or a leaker, depending no less on the power to frame the narrative (Bushnell et al., 2019); the two are often one and the same, depending on a perspective.

[4] https://ec.europa.eu/commission/presscorner/detail/en/MEMO_18_3442   (last accessed August 17, 2022).

[5] https://ec.europa.eu/commission/presscorner/detail/en/MEMO_18_3442   (last accessed August 17, 2022).

ON THE SHIFT FROM WHISTLEBLOWER PROTECTION TO THREAT MANAGEMENT

Already the anticipation of this directive sent the compliance-industrial complex into overdrive—from benchmark reports and surveys, webinars, product brochures, blog posts, perpetual emails asking whether one's organization is ready to comply with the regulation, explaining what it means, including all possible threats and risks connected to non-compliance, to all the marketing of products and services organizations need to purchase to become compliant, from compliant speak-up platforms and case management systems to training. This is not to mention the ISO 37002:2021 *Whistleblowing Management Systems—Guidelines*—work on which coincided with the work on the directive, further enhancing the massive global business of certifying and auditing compliance, along with the business of the many accrediting agencies, such as the 93 accreditation bodies recognized by the International Accreditation Forum (IAF)[6] (for a history of global standard setting and the evolution of managerial standards from technical standards, see: Yates & Murphy, 2019). As industry experts from an American multinational law firm put it,

> These requirements are likely to create logistical complexities not only for companies with a footprint in the EU but also for foreign companies seeking to acquire an EU target or doing business with an EU company. (...) It is likely that, given the potential for member states to go beyond the requirements of the Directive in their whistleblower policies and procedures, companies will approach compliance in a similar way to the AML regime. Companies operating Europe-wide may consider that a gold-plated standard for their whistleblowing policy is the simplest route to ensure both a unified approach across their business as well as compliance with the Directive and differing standards at the national level.[7]

The directive is being interpreted, mediated, and re-interpreted by professionals across space only to be translated by other professionals into a more practical 'gold-plated standard' that promises to satisfy across jurisdictions and result in more efficient compliance, but that also works

[6] https://iaf.nu/en/home/ (last accessed August 17, 2022).

[7] https://www.skadden.com/insights/publications/2021/06/blowing-the-whistle (last accessed August 17, 2022).

on the assumption of the necessity of overcompliance and the magnification of the threat. Quickly, it also becomes unclear whether the bigger threat would stem from the regulators or from the potential whistleblowers, disgruntled employees, and others likely to leak internal information. The irony is that the same compliance systems that are built to comply with anti-retaliation policies do at times turn against the very compliance officers who craft and enforce them. In Kate Kenny's wonderful book on whistleblowing, most of her informants were in fact in charge of risk management, compliance, anti-money laundering, and anti-corruption work in their respective institutions. It was their job to flag and report fraud, suspicious transactions, or unethical behaviours. But their concerns were systematically ignored, and they were actively prevented from performing their duties. The more systemic the corruption and fraud, the more violent the response to raising their concern appeared to be. Kenny even concludes that 'the cruel expulsion of the whistleblower from organizational life, both materially and symbolically, is an important part of business of usual' (Kenny, 2019, p. 116). A former compliance officer, later reframed, against their own will as a whistleblower, similarly remarked that,

> if anything goes wrong, they can simply fire you. That realization after the horrendous prosecution, I had death threats, my family had death threats, over half of the people in my company thought I was evil and that the fraudster was some kind of folk hero, some kind of William Tell, for stealing the company's money. (...) If you object to the corporate view of the world, you become instantly a troublemaker and an outsider. Even though the accepted cultural norm within this organisation is to drive people 24 hours a day and set them unrealistic targets and reward them for high sales. If that is the norm, then if you rail against that, if you object to that, you become an outsider. Good apples stand out in bad barrels, the same way the bad apples stand out in good barrels. If everybody else around you is a pretty rotten apple then it does not pay to be a good apple, you get thrown out; the system rejects you. That could mean, you get fired, you get demoted, you get overlooked when promotion comes, actually get bullied as a whistleblower in the extreme. It is the cultural norms that get set by incentives, and objectives, instantly if you object to those you are an outsider. You have to be terribly brave and terribly confident in your own self to stand up against an organisation when everybody else is going along with that.

The compliance officer, playing both an internal police officer and an ethics champion, can quickly find herself in trouble, victim to the very same systems that he helped implement—being investigated, charged with breaches of ethics. Implementing policies that typically rely on denial of *systemic* fraud (which is, at best, deemed unusual) and promoting the idea of that it is *individual* 'bad apples' that are responsible for fraud and that it is the 'rogue' employee that needs to be identified and surgically removed in order to not spoil the corporate body (Sylvia & Stabile, 2018), can quickly turn against the compliance officer; she may become that very 'rogue'. In the case of Paul Moore, described in Kenny's book in detail, KPMG performed an investigation and wrote a report which criticized his 'disruptive nature' and came with a range of claims about his personality. Others became investigated for minor infringements of company policy, which were nothing compared to the wrongdoings they were addressing (Kenny, 2019). Their ethics, their values, their personality, their behaviour, their thoughts, all were subjected to an investigation. It is worth making the following point here: while many anti-policies, especially those directed at financial crimes, are sold as targeting the powerful, when these become translated into the logic of management, they transmorph into the policing of labour, targeting the individual. In other words, the methods of 'high policing', when refracted through the lens and the apparatus of management, turn into a form of 'low policing'. Despite the spectacular enforcement actions, multi-million-dollar settlements and fines, and the few prosecutions of elite individuals, these enforcement actions inhabit the realm of the extraordinary and rare. Despite their power to shape the discourse, the reality on the ground is one of power and managerial hierarchies, one of power that targets downwards. As Edelman remarks:

> The relentlessness of private policing becomes particularly significant by virtue of its interaction with bureaucratic hierarchy. Because in-house security forces are accountable primarily to management, their legitimacy does not depend on their ability to appear neutral with respect to the organization's stratification system (...) This directional bias may appear in many guises, but perhaps the most consequential is the role that private security forces play in focusing the organizational gaze 'downward,' that is, in exposing the activities of lower-level participants to panoptical surveillance while shrouding the activities of upper-level participants behind a veil of secrecy. (...) In short, private security acts sort of one-way mirror, revealing the activities of subordinates to superiors while obscuring the

activities of superiors from subordinates. Beyond simply mobilizing public law on behalf of private interests, the internalization of law enforcement therefore plays an active part in the construction of a new organizational regime, one that is uniquely responsive to the control of elites and uniquely fortified against the critiques of the public. (Edelman & Suchman, 1999, pp. 975–976)

The hybrid regulatory apparatus, through the work of its legal, technical, security, management, and ethics experts, through its frenetic manufacturing of consensus, standards, best practices, and so on, is in the business of issuing guidelines on how others are to work, think, and feel. It produces the often invisible and increasingly technological structures and architectures of the world others are to inhabit, but of which the rule-maker is often free (to be a rule-breaker). The other is to submit to these dictates, policies, guidelines, and rules and be punished, sanctioned, for any deviance, any breach, any reported or automatically generated notification by the corporate sovereign. In the extreme scenario, the corporate sovereign may even decide in matters of life and death (Jakobsen, 2020; Whyte, 2003).

On Ensuring Compliance Through Pre-Crime and Corporate Security

This enforcement is increasingly envisioned in the terms of compliance and security ensured *through* pre-crime and pre-punishment directed at both external threats and internal threats, such as likely whistleblowers. While the technologies are neither accurate, not as yet thoroughly implemented, this does not mean that they are not being embraced, ideologically, and sold as *the* future. Bogus AI and roboprocesses implemented in the name of these visions are already resulting in new harms and injustices (Besteman & Gusterson, 2019; Eubanks, 2018; Mbadiwe, 2018). The compliance-industrial complex is creating its own roboprocesses, those of control of control (of control) for the sake of control, of risk scoring that generates suspicion and of manufacturing of threats.

The conjuncture between computerization and neoliberalism has produced roboprocesses skewed in favor of corporate profit making, mass surveillance, and the retrenchment of racial and class-based inequalities. The result has been automated phone systems and checkout systems in stores that frustrate customers but enable corporations to increase profits by laying off staff; a shadowy and unaccountable empire of companies selling profiles of consumers, patients, and borrowers; a justice system whose algorithms disproportionately penalize racial minorities and the poor; workplaces that judge their employees not for their individual achievements but for their degree of conformity to an algorithmic approximation of the ideal employee. (Gusterson, 2019, p. 7)

Algorithmic compliance and management are sold on the market as *the* desirable visions of the future. Books like *AI Revolution in HRM: The New Scorecard* promise a future where

with time, AI will personalize every stage of an employee's life cycle. In the future, AI will manage the preferences for office settings and will plan the day and calendar of employees. AI will also open work files on the basis of deadlines and commitments, taking into account the importance and urgency of the project. In the future, AI will handle sensitive issues such as grievances, terminations and resignations. AI will make the HR function more agile and will enable HR managers in taking quick and relevant insights-driven decisions. (…) With predictive analytics, AI can predict the likelihood of applicant's success. Using data on employee personality types, skills and education, companies can plan the career progression of employees. (Upadhyay et al., 2021, p. 223)

The compliance-industrial complex, as we have seen, is best understood within the framework of pluralization and privatization of policing: starting from anti-corruption, anti-money laundering, anti-fraud, via anti-harassment to inappropriate behaviours to breaches of ethical codes, compliance is instrumental in internal policing, investigations, and sanctioning of both legal and ethical breaches, but even critical utterances which may pose reputational risks and threats of reputational damage. The intelligence-led securitized and criminalized compliance as a mode of governance—both within organizations and of the social on behalf of the state—blurs the boundaries between the legal and the ethical and resulting in the hybridization of both criminal law and/or *imitation* thereof as well as of intelligence practices. This undermines the rule of law for those subject to private investigations and pre-emptive intelligence-led management systems and (semi-)automated 'roboprocesses' (Besteman & Gusterson, 2019), which make recourse to justice increasingly difficult. These systems, driven by the logic of risk management, aim not only to manage and control but often also eliminate both external and internal threats *before* they materialize, as well as punish and sanction. Both external and internal actors are seen primarily as suspects and as guilty until proven innocent, where this innocence can at any moment flip into the opposite and therefore requires permanent monitoring and surveillance. Employees are seen as risk, as a potential (criminal) liability, as do suppliers, and other third parties. Therefore, all need to be screened, authorized, authenticated, validated, the patterns of their behaviour evaluated and assessed, any deviance from what is deemed 'normal' (or their personalized normal) is flagged, turning into a *suspicion*. And since compliance aims not only to ensure that legal obligations are being followed, but also to instil a culture of compliance, of ethics, it tends to increasingly fuse with human resource management. The RegTech industry is growing, along with other providers of managerial technosolutions. Compliance taps increasingly into both the knowledge and power of HRM and overlays these systems with its logic of policing (or, alternatively, it reveals the true colours of HRM as *the* instrument of policing labour, this power now only being expanded also to those outside the organization). With the rise of big data and artificial intelligence, and the demands for effectivization, cost-efficiency, and for data-driven and evidence-based decision-making, both compliance and HRM are being platformized, which further increases their integration. The practices and rhetoric of 'intelligence', 'forensic evidence', 'real-time monitoring', 'investigations', 'threat assessments', and so forth, which borrow from the police and the military, lurk behind the glossy brochures about 'ethical corporate culture'. Compliance platforms increasingly imitate predictive policing and other data-driven intelligence tools. The trend is decidedly one of moving away from reactive rule-based automated solutions, which merely detect breaches of these rules or policies, towards proactive data-driven pre-emptive detection of anomalies and 'bad behaviours', seen as potential indicators of future breaches and towards a real-time '360 view' of situations and persons.[8]

---

[8] An interested reader may for instance listen to the following industry conversation: https://podcasts.apple.com/us/podcast/how-automation-ai-are-changing-the-com pliance-officer-role/id1479203122?i=1000575420414 (last accessed August 15, 2022).

These practices have been traditionally tied to corporate security, which has evolved historically from its violent forms of labour coercion, via physical security, corporate security, and IT security, to 'total asset protection', 'where protection of tangible and intangible assets as well as a more global outlook came to characterize corporate security.' Within this paradigm, 'every employee, every object – from stapler to semi-truck – and every fragment of information is conceived as an asset and risk', and 'corporate and organizational interests align with security. Security managers are brought in to executive decision-making' (Walby & Lippert, 2014b, p. 6). Following the professionalization of corporate security experts, and the proliferation of security standards, codes of conduct, and so on, we see similar professionalization of compliance. Compliance in this sense legitimizes corporate security and its actions in the name of anti-policies, which appear to transgress the narrow interests of the corporation and which, in the logic of stakeholder capitalism and ethical business, can provide a reputational veneer of doing good. Moreover, compliance legitimizes the application of the techniques of corporate security onto the realm of ethics and values. As such, it not only legitimizes governance *through* security (Walby & Lippert, 2014a), but also the securitization of the 'governance of the soul' (Rose, 1999). Furthermore, it legitimizes the integration of HR into the apparatus of corporate security—in the name of compliance. It explicitly encourages holistic and integrated approaches that transgress the organizational silos, such as those between HR and the corporate security apparatus. It is precisely here that the RegTechs find their markets, as this integration often takes the form of data integration and platformization. Even Microsoft has developed its own solution in the form of Microsoft Purview, which merges risk and compliance and data governance; while much is related to the management of data assets, focus is also directed at insider threat management and communication compliance which promise to 'detect code of conduct violations (including harassing or threatening language, adult content, and sharing sensitive information)'.[9] At the same time, the state, through anti-policies and regulations that demand compliance and intelligence production for the authorities, can extend its authority and exploit the power of the corporate security-cum-compliance apparatus and platforms,

---

[9] https://www.microsoft.com/security/blog/2022/04/19/the-future-of-compliance-and-data-governance-is-here-introducing-microsoft-purview/ (last accessed August 20, 2022).

without being responsible for their actions and consequences. In the next chapter, we continue this discussion by looking closer at the role of expertise in the compliance-industrial complex and later on, we shall see how it is being built into algorithmic architectures.

REFERENCES

Besteman, C., & Gusterson, H. (Eds.). (2019). *Life by algorithms: How roboprocesses are remaking our world*. University of Chicago Press. https://doi.org/10.7208/chicago/9780226627731.001.0001

Birkenfeld, B. C. (2020). *Lucifer's banker: Uncensored*. Republic Book Publishers.

Bushnell, A., Kenny, K., & Fotaki, M. (2019). The battle for the whistleblower: An interview with John Kiriakou. *Ephemera: Theory & Politics in Organization, 19*(4), 829–850.

Ceva, E., & Bocchiola, M. (2019). *Is whistleblowing a duty?* Polity.

Edelman, L. B., & Suchman, M. C. (1999). When the 'haves' hold court: Speculations on the organizational internalization of law. *Law & Society Review, 33*(4), 941–991. https://doi.org/10.2307/3115155

Eubanks, V. (2018). *Automating inequality: How high-tech tools profile*. St. Martin's Press.

Glasbeek, H. (2002). *Wealth by stealth: Corporate crime, corporate law, and the perversion of democracy*. Between the Lines.

Gray, G. G. (2006). The regulation of corporate violations: Punishment, compliance, and the blurring of responsibility. *British Journal of Criminology, 46*, 875–892. https://doi.org/10.1093/bjc/azl005

Gusterson, H. (2019). Introduction: Robohumans. In C. Besteman & H. Gusterson (Eds.), *Life by algorithms: How roboprocesses are remaking our world* (pp. 1–30). University of Chicago Press. https://doi.org/10.7208/chicago/9780226627731.003.0001

Jakobsen, L. J. (2020). Corporate security technologies: Managing life and death along a Colombian coal railway. *Political Geography, 83*. https://doi.org/10.1016/j.polgeo.2020.102273

Kenny, K. (2019). Whistleblowing: Toward a new theory. *Harvard University Press*. https://doi.org/10.4159/9780674239715

Kenny, K., Fotaki, M., & Scriver, S. (2019). Mental health as a weapon: Whistleblower retaliation and normative violence. *Journal of Business Ethics, 160*, 801–815. https://doi.org/10.1007/s10551-018-3868-4

Kristeva, J. (1982). *Powers of horror: An essay on abjection*. Columbia University Press.

Kuldova, T. Ø., & Nordrik, B. (Forthcoming). Workplace investigations and the hollowing out of the Norwegian model of co-determination. *Class and Capital*.

Mbadiwe, T. (2018). Algorithmic injustice. *The New Atlantis: A Journal of Technology & Society, Winter*, 3–28.

Nordrik, B., & Kuldova, T. Ø. (2021). *Faktaundersøkelser—et "hybrid konfliktvåpen" på norske arbeidsplasser.* Gyldendal Akademisk.

Rose, N. (1999). *Governing the soul: The shaping of the private self.* Free Association Books.

Sampson, S. (2019). Citizen duty or stasi society? Whistleblowing and disclosure regimes in organizations and communities. *Ephemera: Theory & Politics in Organizations, 19*(4), 777–806.

Sylvia, C., & Stabile, E. (2018). Rethinking compliance: The role of whistleblowers. *University of Cincinnati Law Review, 84*(2), 451–474.

Upadhyay, A., Khandelwal, K., & Iyengar, J. (2021). AI Revolution in HRM: The New scorecard. *SAGE.* https://doi.org/10.4135/9789354792861

Vandekerckhove, W., & Tsahuridu, E. E. (2010). Risky rescues and the duty to blow the whistle. *Journal of Business Ethics, 97*(3), 365–380. https://doi.org/10.1007/s10551-010-0513-2

Walby, K., & Lippert, R. K. (2014a). Corporate security in the 21st century: Theory and practice in international perspective. *Palgrave Macmillan.* https://doi.org/10.1057/9781137346070

Walby, K., & Lippert, R. K. (2014b). Introduction: governing every person, place, and thing—Critical studies of corporate security. In K. Walby & R. K. Lippert (Eds.), *Corporate security in the 21st century: Theory and practice in international perspective* (pp. 1–16). Palgrave Macmillan. https://doi.org/10.1057/9781137346070_1

Whyte, D. (2003). Lethal regulation: State-corporate crime and the United Kingdom government's new mercenaries. *Journal of Law and Society, 30*(4), 575–600. https://doi.org/10.1111/j.1467-6478.2003.00271.x

Yates, J., & Murphy, C. N. (2019). *Engineering rules: Global standard setting since 1880* John Hopkins University Press.

CHAPTER 6

Compliance-Industrial Complex and Its Experts

Abstract We look closer at the particular forms of expertise and knowledge that inform compliance, and the technocratic and algorithmic architectures built to deliver it. We reflect on the fetishization of data and transparency and on flawed visions of objectivity and neutrality—and on consensus building and multistakeholderism. We look at the struggles for professional legitimacy and the translation of particular forms of expertise (at the expense of others) into the currency of private and voluntary self-regulation, standardization, and standard setting which promise to deliver *universal* 'best practices'. We consider how come that the repeated failures of these forms of expertise only stimulate demand for *more* of the same—for more control, more compliance, more rules, more guidelines—rather than a serious rethinking of these practices.

Keywords ISO standards · Technical expertise · Best practice · Consultocracy · Uncontrollability

The compliance-industrial complex is built around expertise. It is built around converging and *compatible* forms of expertise: law and human resource management, risk management, accounting, but also IT security and big data analytics, statistical modelling, psychometrics, neoclassical

© The Author(s), under exclusive license to Springer Nature   97
Switzerland AG 2022
T. Ø. Kuldova, *Compliance-Industrial Complex*,
https://doi.org/10.1007/978-3-031-19224-1_6

and behavioural economics, policing, intelligence, security, and engineering. Even Taylor would possibly not imagine that the market in scientific management (Taylor, 1919) would grow to these proportions—and that managerial techniques, accounting, governance by numbers and digital Taylorism (Dewinter et al., 2014; Glover, 2013) would underpin the go to solutions to global crime, social and environmental problems. These forms of knowledge do not only valorise, but *fetishize* concepts such as objectivity, neutrality, due process, transparency and so on, and not least *data*. A critical understanding of the social construction of data, of risk, of the messy processes that go into the supposedly neutral and technological solutions, are largely completely absent. In many ways, these forms of expert knowledge aim to 'manufacture rationality' (Shenhav, 2007), using data and sleek data visualizations to support these expert architectures. Instead, they are more accurately conceived as 'technologies of speculation' that tend to disavow the limits of data-driven knowledge (Hong, 2020). But it is precisely these limits that provoke speculative processes that put uncertainties, flawed models, flaky numbers, prejudiced estimates, or dubious correlations to work in an attempt to satisfy the desire for and fantasy of epistemic purity and visions of technological objectivity, rationality, and certainty (Hong, 2020). But the valorisation of expertise and data in the governance of human affairs is neither natural or given; it is a result of a long historical process as much as struggles of managerial experts to make themselves relevant, a history where both capital owners and employees initially resisted the engineering experts. Or as Shenhav describes the antecedents of the so called 'managerial revolution':

> Lacking their own means of production, engineers could only offer their engineering principles in order to gain respectable position in the industrial order. Moreover, they encountered opposition from manufacturers who were apprehensive about the introduction of managerial methods. Manufacturers viewed the attempt to invent management practices as a strategy employed by engineers to expand their professional territory. To them, management systems were costly and superfluous. At the other pole of the capitalist order, the proletariats were forming their interests, strategies, and representatives. They, too, rejected engineering-based managerial ideas. (…) In the initial opposition of both many employers and the employees to the rise of management, labor unrest was introduced as a leverage to gain legitimacy for management practices. They eventually

played a significant role in redefining it (after 1900) from a war of attri-
tion between owners and crafts to a mere tension between 'management',
'employees', and 'professionals'. They did so by colonizing the discourse
and monopolizing industrial know-how. (...) They became the priests
of organizational rationality, mobilizing business ideology around secular
engineering ideals rather than previously dominant religious, philanthropic,
or Social Darwinist theories. 'Systems' and 'systematization,' were concep-
tualized as ideological tropes. Engineers' efforts reproduced the ideological
assumption that human and non-human entities are interchangeable and
can be equally subjected to engineering manipulation. (Shenhav, 2007,
pp. 18–19; emphasis mine)

The engineers 'manufacturing rationality' in the world of business, and
later on, through New Public Management (NPM) in the public sector
as well (Craig et al., 2014; Hansen et al., 2002), eventually won, along
with their 'quality management systems' underpinning all ISO managerial
standards (Yates & Murphy, 2019) to their conceptions of the 'human',
now not only engineerable, but within the cybernetic imaginary also
programmable (Supiot, 2017). Technocratic approaches to governance
that view the world as *programmable*, the human and the social as *quantifiable*, and thus as controllable through different modes of *anticipatory*
data-driven governance have become hegemonic (Hong, 2020).

Futuristic imaginaries of posthuman augmentation and absolute predic-
tivity endow today's imperfect machines with a sense of legitimacy. In the
process, technologies of datafication are reshaping what counts as knowledge in their own image (...) redefining what kinds of data in whose hands
should determine the truth of who I am or what is good for me. (Hong,
2020, pp. 1–2)

These systems are thus geared in many ways towards the manufacturing
of suspicion in the name of rationality, or under its guise. The same
forms of knowledge production underpin pre-crime *imaginaries*, such
as those manifest in techniques of intelligence-led policing, private and
public. Not only the limits of the data, but also the role of imagination
is typically disavowed, and 'denied in the implementation of pre-crime.
The language of science, mathematics, police and intelligence expertise
and political authority is used to mask the central place of imagination
in pre-crime' (McCulloch & Wilson, 2016, p. 8). Despite the promises
of 'targeted governance in which security decisions are finely calibrated

towards specific threats and problems' (McCulloch & Wilson, 2016, p. 80), and despite the visions of the future as one of data-driven 'personalization of law', with different rules for different people based on their behavioural patterns, cognitive abilities, and predicted reactions (Ben-Shahar & Porat, 2021), these systems tend to create a formalized, flat, one-dimensional (Marcuse, 1964), and positive world. Through the aligned logic of *pre-crime*—all deviance, negativity, and resistance, all friction, dissent, emotion, all informality, and even the quirkiness of simply being human—are to be erased in favour of formalized positivity and harmony. Any friction, any disharmony, is to be eliminated. These approaches have won through in the *long durée* battle of ideas that has led to what Beniger analysed as the 'control revolution' (Beniger, 1986); they have won at the expense of alternative approaches—not least because they align well with the interests of capital. The global governance of crime and the fight against transnational organized crime has not only been at the centre of development of these technocratic architectures (Nieto Martín, 2022), but it has also shaped their logic.

ON THE STRUGGLE FOR PROFESSIONAL LEGITIMACY

Struggles over which knowledge will become hegemonic are often the struggles of professions seeking markets, power, and legitimacy. This was the case for personnel managers, for fraud experts and it is the case for compliance professionals. Williams described nicely how 'forensic accounting' and the fraud detection experts, very much integral to the compliance-industrial complex, worked hard to establish themselves as relevant professional actors, underlining, too, the dramatic growth 'training and certification programs and accompanying texts, manuals and how-to-guides' since the 1990s (Williams, 2014, p. 59). Williams shows the ways in which forensic accountants actively created not only a mythology around their profession, but also established forensic accounting as 'a specialized and well-defined body of expert knowledge' and how they have claimed 'professional jurisdiction over the practice area of fraud detection and investigation'. In the process, and much in line with the aforementioned tendencies, they have not only shaped the understanding of the 'fraud problem' but also recast 'fraud as primarily committed by employees', involving 'activities such as theft of information or misappropriation of corporate assets by lower-level employees rather than senior managers and executives' (Williams, 2014, p. 61), thus understanding fraud primarily through the lens of individual vices, moral failures, deviance, and abnormality. As Williams also notes, the forensic accounting and corporate investigation industry (FACI) is 'geared first and foremost toward the construction of a market for its services which involves problematizing and dramatizing fraud but in a way that is likely to resonate with, and appeal to, corporate decision-makers' (Williams, 2014, p. 64). The compliance professionals have followed similar trajectory, one of actively crafting their legitimacy and their expertise. This form of expertise also tends to exaggerate compliance risks and expand the logic of fraud, risk, and employee misconduct, consequently integrating fraud expertise under the umbrella of compliance.

The compliance-industrial complex centres around a growing training and certification industry. Every new regulation, every new standard, every new guideline—often already created by relying on the non-transparent and informal work of technical experts and range of bodies such as the Financial Action Task Force (FATF), shaping the international AML/CFT regulatory regime through recommendations and guidance (Tilahun, 2021)—translates into the need for staff training, for updated knowledge, or a new software product which, too, demands training sessions and continuous follow-up and evaluations. A transnational community of 'financial crime fighters' and 'ethical champions' has emerged, brought together by these training sessions, courses, certifications, compliance conferences, and an endless stream of webinars, where professionals collect CPE (continuous professional education) points, renew their certifications (many of which are subscription based, forcing you to pay to keep your certification valid), and where knowledge takes the form of latest regulatory updates, updated best practice responding to 'evolving threats and risks' and the 'rapidly changing regulatory landscape', often combined with a sales pitch for a software or consultancy services. Among the prominent actors on this market are organizations such as ACAMS,[1] Certified Financial Crime Specialists (ACFCS),[2] and a range of compliance academies such as SCCE (Society for Corporate Compliance and Ethics)[3] or the International Compliance Association

---

[1] https://www.acams.org/en (last accessed May 5, 2022).

[2] https://www.acfcs.org/all-news/ (last accessed May 5, 2022).

[3] https://www.corporatecompliance.org/conferences/academies (last accessed May 5, 2022).

(ICA), with many others specializing on concrete industries. There are news sites, magazines such as Compliance Week, blogs such as FCPA + , the Wall Street Journal has dedicated Risk & Compliance section, and so on, in addition to all the trainings offered by the Big Four and similar, various online course providers, and so on. Among those offering popular webinars with CPE credits are companies providing compliance solutions as well as RegTechs, be it Navex Global, Traliant, Thompson Reuters, Speeki, ClauseMatch, and many others.

This expertise is for the most part concentrated in the private sector: where public financial intelligence units in most countries remain under-staffed, subject to austerity measures and budgetary cuts, the private sector supplies a growing fleet of experts and shapes the expertise on the subjects, large banks having hundreds of staff in various AML/CFT and compliance functions, as do audit firms. Not only does this result in a situation where the suspects effectively investigate themselves,[4] but they also concentrate the very knowledge production about finan-cial crimes and compliance in their hands. This knowledge, which has evolved as a response to the AML/CFT regulatory frameworks, has since been expanding to the realms of anti-corruption, human rights violations, slave labour, sexual harassment, and now most prominently ESG, spreading from serving largely financial services and increasingly real estate and health care, to catering to all sorts of businesses. While there are specialists cultivating these distinct areas, the trend—via datafication and platformization—is again to merge these forms of expertise, precisely in response to the expanding risk universe described earlier. Moreover, this expert knowledge crafted by and for the corporate sector in many ways, for voluntary self-regulation, for CSR, for reputation management, is then fed back to the regulatory bodies, eventually contributing to the shaping of regulation, and even practices of public police and FIUs.

Most knowledge producers in the realms of compliance spaces are lawyers, auditors, accountants, managers, human resource managers, psychologists, and of course IT experts. Despite embracing proud labels

---

[4] See, for instance, the description here of the situation in Norway, where the local Financial Intelligence Unit is massively outnumbered by the private sector investigators, both within and outside organizations, and where prosecutions for financial crime are notoriously low: https://forskning.no/finans-kriminalitet-politikk/politiet-overlater-etterf orskningen-av-okonomisk-kriminalitet-til-de-mistenkte/1841798 (last accessed August 20, 2022).

as 'crime fighters' or experts on 'culture', there are few if any criminologists, sociologists, or anthropologists. Accounting and management put in service of crime fighting is one of the dominant paradigms, but it also means that only that which can be accounted for is seen as legitimate (Ala & Lapsley, 2019)—this despite the prominent role of intermediaries, such as accountants in high-end money laundering schemes. There are indeed many former police and intelligence officers, now rebranded as consultants, which typically bring with them, again, the narrow focus on individuals and cases.

Overall, these perspectives do not permit any larger, organizational, and systemic questions—be it about conceptualizations of risk, about the causes of fraud and crime, or critical perspectives on data, power, culture, and inequality. They do not permit *reflexivity* about one's practice (beyond vague talk about ethics) in the context of larger socio-economic structures. The knowledge production on matters of white-collar crime, corruption, financial crimes, terrorism financing, and now even environmental crime, slave labour or human trafficking—and how to combat them, is being effectively captured by a particular set of perspectives that see data-driven compliance in various iterations as the solution.

Accounting, risk management and corporate security align around the overlapping perspectives of formalization, individualization, psychologization, datafication, and quantification. These one-dimensional perspectives again align themselves well with the control functions, where the generation of risk ratings and indicators offers the comforts of numbers. The preferred solution appears to be the building of hostile algorithmic architectures and surveillance systems that profile, rate and rank, while integrating insights from the psy-complex and relying on harvested OSINT data. These experts have definitional power, one that can be purchased and strategically utilized in corporate interest, or as one of my informants put it:

> it is becoming a major industry, there are investigators and there are consultants, ex-law enforcement and ex-intelligence officers. It can be commissioned in a way where they are given the answer at the beginning. Here is what we want you to conclude, we are quite happy to give you hundreds of thousands of pounds to do the investigation as long as you conclude that. I am paraphrasing, but I have seen it happen. And I have seen objectives set. You were overseeing conclusion and you see it repeatedly in the financial services world. ...the internal investigation business is

big, but the regulator is driving that. One of the problems for the regulator is that he does not have enough money to do his own investigations.

Along with the power of these knowledge producers, comes the power of so-called technical experts and committees producing standards.

On ISO Standards
and the Manufacturing of Consensus

Private standardization organizations, such as ISO, play a key role in supporting these hegemonic forms of global governance and are themselves important players. Easterling analysed ISO as a form of 'extrastatecraft', which sets the premises for both visible and invisible architectures and infrastructures of governance (Easterling, 2016). International organizations like ISO, consultancy and audit companies, and the compliance-industrial complex at large, hence like to present themselves as *apolitical*, *neutral*, and *non-partisan*. They frame their work in terms of *technical expertise* and specialized knowledge relying on *consensus* and broad expert validation through technical and expert committees and complex and expensive bureaucratic processes that generate 'best practice' (to be continually improved and updated). They succeed in presenting themselves as 'merely technical' despite their deeply political missions that exclude forms of knowledge that contest the hegemonic narratives. Alternatively, they simply co-opt critique through participative processes, where participating in a process equals putting one's name on and thus legitimizing the final product (Louis & Maertens, 2021).

There is possibly no better example of this than ISO, the private standard setting organization with its international and national bodies, thousands of committees and complex bureaucratic processes relying on 'experts' and expert 'stakeholders' to craft the highly rigid but also general standards—some of the most popular in the field of quality management. The ISO/TC 309 *Governance of Organizations* technical committee has, for instance, developed the recent ISO 37301:2021 *Compliance Management Systems* and ISO 37002:2021 *Whistleblowing Management Systems*, as well as the ISO 37001:2016 *Anti-Bribery Management Systems*, and a number of others—declaring standards a way to combat corruption, helping to make the UN Global Agenda 2030 and its SDG goals a reality.[5] It is here that vague principles become translated into more concrete guidance for practice and into products (such as compliance software) that align with these standards; the structure of these standards thus impacts the shape of anti-corruption and compliance in organizations. They become celebrated as important international benchmarks and a 'resource that governments can leverage in their evaluation' as Microsoft's Legal Compliance Programs Director remarked when praising the ISO 37001:2016.[6]

While it is said that any expert or relevant stakeholder is invited to participate in the development of standards, and that standards rely on a consensus-based democratic process, the reality is more complicated. Participation is often prohibitively expensive and time-consuming, requiring one to fly around the globe (Forsberg, 2012), which is often too big of an expense for public interest organizations, smaller NGOs, watchdogs, and other civil society actors. Large corporations often have dedicated positions and actively invest in the development of standards, which indeed translate into new markets. But 'best practice' is not only shaped by funds and power, but also by the same logic of codes of conduct. Or rather, these ensure that any fundamental critique is excluded. To participate in any of the technical committee's one must sign under the *Code of Conduct for the Technical Work*[7] and the *ISO Code of Ethics*,[8] a matter that has been emphasized numerous times during the course in standardization that I attended, which would qualify me for participation in the national (shadow) committee. What this means is that one must effectively sign on that one agrees with the goals of standardization and considers standardization an unquestioned social good, will actively promote the implementation of these standards, and 'will not hinder their development'.[9] Examples have been given of individuals who raised 'unproductive critique' and attempted to challenge the system and the logic of standards from within. These have been exemplarily dismissed

---

[5] https://www.iso.org/news/ref2772.html (last accessed April 22, 2022).

[6] https://www.iso.org/news/ref2238.html (last accessed August 20, 2022).

[7] https://www.iso.org/files/live/sites/isoorg/files/store/en/PUB100397.pdf (last accessed April 27, 2022).

[8] https://www.iso.org/files/live/sites/isoorg/files/archive/pdf/en/codeethics_2004-en.pdf (last accessed April 27, 2022).

[9] https://www.iso.org/files/live/sites/isoorg/files/store/en/PUB100397.pdf (last accessed April 27, 2022).

from their voluntary and self-financed participation on charges of breach of the ethical code and code of conduct. 'Consensus' is thus built either through co-option or expulsion.

Relying on multistakeholderism, ISO is a prime example of a techno-bureaucratic legitimatory system that encourages participation and involvement to gain legitimacy, but rarely listens to dissenting voices. The committees are disproportionately populated by industry interests (Graz, 2018), as in the case of the aforementioned standards, where the Big Four and other consultancy and audit companies are said to account for the majority of 'technical experts' and have enough resources to travel and dedicate time to the development of standards. This is an example of a system that tends to stifle

> legitimate dissent from external actors who have no interest in lending legitimacy to the façade of an apolitical negotiation. By linking legitimacy to the inclusion of all stakeholders, pressure is exerted on actors to get involved, leaving very little place to legitimately criticize the outcomes of negotiations. (Powers & Jablonski, 2015, p. 24)

One is, in fact, bound by codes of conduct that prevent public critique of outcomes. Once signed, one cannot utter oneself critically about a standard in the public sphere. Upon realizing that by participating in the process of standardization I would neither be able to influence the standard in any serious way—due to the pre-defined high-level structure and standardized definitions of key concepts, the complex and expensive bureaucratic processes, and the disproportionate power of corporate stakeholders—nor be able to publish any critical insights on the process in retrospect, or even criticize any of the standards, I concluded that the participation is incompatible with academic freedom and that expertise of those who participate—irrespective of their position—is used to legitimize this private product and generate an perception of consensus. And yet, this private product is written into laws and regulations across the world and sells itself as stemming from a *democratic* (because participatory) multistakeholder processes governed by ethical codes and best practice. These standards that cannot be disputed become the default settings for organizations: staff is trained in their logic, organizational compliance with standards is certified, and now they are even seen as the best practice for tackling corruption.

There is thus a global knowledge industry shaping and standardizing not only the future of work (Bartley, 2005, 2011), but governance itself—as compliance. As a knowledge industry, the compliance-industrial complex increasingly shapes the limits of the thinkable in the realm of governance of the social. Paraphrasing Fisher's 'capitalist realism' (Fisher, 2009) and the impossibility to imagine alternatives to capitalism, we could coin the term 'compliance realism' as its interlinked derivative. Compliance realism is not in any sense natural and given but is actively created and daily reproduced by a multitude of powerful market players, lobbyists, standardization and industry bodies, national and transnational governance bodies, and civil society actors through networked and hybrid global governance (Graz, 2018; Nieto Martín, 2022).

This knowledge market of the compliance-industrial complex is also heavily invested in creating and manufacturing reputations, valued on the stock market, and in the prevention of reputational damage and its increasing costs. After all, following the Petrobras corruption scandal in Brazil, in which the company agreed to paying settlements with Brazilian and US authorities worth $853,2 million in 2018, it was compliance and integrity programs that were credited with bringing the company back to life after the company built up a massive corporate debt.[10] The Petrobras compliance program reads as a mixture of leading global best practices on steroids, all that is deemed desirable is combined—as per the non-prosecution agreement with DOJ.[11] It can also be noted that DOJ recognized the company as a *victim*, stating that 'a number of executives of the company engaged in an embezzlement scheme that victimized the company and its shareholders'.[12] The compliance program, while imposed, has been key in improving the company's reputation. The certified knowledge can thus be turned into reputational capital. The amount of capital and time that is channelled into building reputations, which can be—in the networked world of social media—destroyed in seconds, is a form of capital that needs to be protected by the organization at all

---

[10] https://www.wsj.com/articles/perfect-storm-at-petrobras-the-worlds-most-indebted-oil-company-1447944976 (last accessed August 19, 2022).

[11] https://www.wsj.com/articles/petrobras-concludes-bribery-settlement-with-u-s-justice-department-11633450508 (last accessed August 19, 2022).

[12] https://www.justice.gov/opa/pr/petr-leo-brasileiro-sa-petrobras-agrees-pay-more-850-million-fcpa-violations (last accessed August 19, 2022).

costs. Hence, the securitization and criminalization of compliance, inclusive of the securitization of critical utterances, and even of emotions and 'micro-aggressions'.

On the Failures that Stimulate the Quest for More of the Same

Despite all this certified expertise, big data, and latest AI-powered tools, it is questionable to what degree the compliance-industrial complex succeeds in its crime prevention and policing tasks. Or at the least, its failure is often openly proclaimed by governments, multilateral bodies, and industry actors alike, despite the simultaneous celebrations of progress. The anti-money laundering, anti-corruption, and compliance architectures have been time and again declared ineffective and utter failures, in particular when judging by the number of money launderers actually brought to justice, and the tiny fraction of laundered money ever recovered (Bullough, 2022; Pol, 2020; Verhage, 2011). Pol even concludes that

> the anti-money laundering policy intervention has less than 0.1 percent impact on criminal finances, compliance costs exceed recovered criminal funds more than a hundred times over, and banks, taxpayers and ordinary citizens are penalized more than criminal enterprises. (Pol, 2020, p. 73)

These repeated failures have, however, only further stimulated the frenetic quest for *more* of the same. Control architectures become layered on top of each other resulting in layers of delegated governance and responsibility and different forms of governance by proxy (Elkin-Koren & Haber, 2016), where it becomes increasingly impossible to tell who governs whom, how, to what effect and who is ultimately accountable or where justice is to be had.

While much debate is waged about the efficiency of these systems, their costs, their possible improvements—or else, again, much of the debate boils down to technical issues and technical fixes, less attention is paid to what kind of society these systems of governance are bringing to life. While these systems appear not particularly effective in catching and prosecuting systemic, complex, transnational, layered, elite crime, and corruption, nor in generating ethical corporate cultures, they are indeed effective in creating increasingly harmonized and standardized global governance, control architectures and moral regulations. These control architectures have universal ambitions—this is why they rely on formalism, legalism, deontology, quantification of risk, and other ever-proliferating metrics and indicators (Merry, 2011, 2020). They make the world measurable, comparable, rateable, and thus flat; they make it submit to a unified vision of governance—underpinned by a unified vision of deviance, where informality tends to translate into a risk for illegality and where any country, organization, and increasingly persons, can be benchmarked, compared, ranked, assessed, through the same standard. For all the talk of diversity, it is uniformity which is being systematically pursued—deviance from the *average* which is considered a 'norm' is labelled as abnormality and something to be punished.

These systems are also strikingly empty, despite their statistical and processual refinements. They are far more open to both interpretation and arbitrary rule-creation than one would admit. For all the talk of guidelines, processes, procedures, and documentation that one needs to have in place, the *actual content*, the actual ways of calculating risk, tend to be often evaded in the discussions by compliance professionals. The focus on structure and form dominates and questions of substance are glossed over in passing. With the rise of machine learning, it even becomes legitimate to delegate the actual content to the machine, as it searches for patters only the machine is deemed to understand, patterns beyond human understanding, but patterns of suspicion and deviance nonetheless; the authority over content is delegated to patterns, which acquire a peculiar authority of their own (Kaufmann et al., 2018). This emptiness of formalism and institutionalism is, however, key to their power and key to the enforcement of 'good governance'. The frenetic proliferation of these increasingly impenetrable regulatory, control, audit, and compliance architectures (despite being built in the name of transparency) can be viewed as a manic proliferation of structures of disavowal that effectively enable the continuation of 'business as usual' including all the tax havens in offshore jurisdictions (Bullough, 2022), corporate fraud, exploitation of workers, of the environment and of 'gangster capitalism' at large (Woodiwiss, 2005). They are thus more worth for their *performative* effects of frenetically staging accountability and morality—in their absence. This apparatus thus relies on performance of hegemonic knowledge that legitimizes itself as universal and inherently good—be it the aforementioned best practices or the illusions of technological neutrality and objectivity; both trends aligned in their self-proclaimed apolitical and technocratic posture.

In this light, the compliance-industrial complex can be seen as a peculiar result of 'modernity's incessant desire to make the world engineerable, predictable, available, accessible, disposable (i.e. *verfügbar*) in all its aspects'. In the process, however, as Rosa observes,

> this desire for control produces, behind our backs, a world that in the end is utterly uncontrollable in all the relevant aspects. We cannot control our late modern world in any way: politically, economically, legally, technologically, or individually. The drive and desire toward controllability ultimately creates monstrous, frightening forms of uncontrollability. (Rosa, 2021, pp. viii–ix)

Not only do these proliferating architectures of control result in colossal uncontrollability and even more uncontrollable unintended consequences, but they also largely appear to fail to deliver on their declared intentions. These failures, however, do not stimulate rethinking, but instead a constant demand for *more*—more data, more regulation, more guidelines, more rules, more surveillance, more reporting, more audit, more accountability measures, more standardization, more ratings, more indicators, more frameworks, and so on—or else, different forms of more in the service of control. This has created a monstrous world of information overload (*more* leaks and more data) accompanied by an absence of meaning; a 'technopoly' where it becomes nearly impossible to make a principled argument and raise fundamental questions (Postman, 1993). Technocratic expert architectures and infrastructures wrapped in 'techno-strategic language' (Cohn, 1987) pushed by the high priests of 'consultocracy' (Ylönen & Kuusela, 2019) and 'regulocracy' (Sataøen, 2018) effectively exclude anyone who does not *submit* to and comply with their written and unwritten rules. One may use words like 'greenwashing' about ESG investments, or 'compliance washing'— but a multibillion-dollar compliance and 'information-industrial complex' stands in the way of any such critique being taken seriously. This complex indoctrinates, rewards compliance, prevents genuine understanding, paralyzes dissent, and disorients populations at scale. How could one be against expertise and best practice, after all they have both morality and the best certified and accredited knowledge on their side? In the next chapter, which is also the last, we shall turn to the promises of artificial intelligence and RegTech and the reader will be able to deduce some more reasons as to why we should resist uncritical uptake of these regulatory ideas, expert systems, and technologies.

REFERENCES

Ala, A. S., & Lapsley, I. (2019). Accounting for crime in the neoliberal world. *The British Accounting Review, 51*(5). https://doi.org/10.1016/j.bar.2019.100839

Bartley, T. (2005). Corporate accountability and the privatization of labor standards: Struggles over codes of conduct in the apparel industry. *Research in Political Sociology,* 211–244. https://doi.org/10.1016/S0895-9935(05)14007-8

Bartley, T. (2011). Transnational governance as the layering of rules: Intersections of public and private standards. *Theoretical Inquiries in Law, 12*(2), 517–542. https://doi.org/10.2202/1565-3404.1278

Ben-Shahar, O., & Porat, A. (2021). Personalized law: Different rules for different people. *Oxford University Press.* https://doi.org/10.1093/oso/9780197522813.001.0001

Beniger, J. R. (1986). *The control revolution: Technological and economic origins of the information society.* Harvard University Press.

Bullough, O. (2022). *Butler to the world: How Britain became the servant of Tycoons, Tax Dodgers.* Profile Books.

Cohn, C. (1987). Sex and death in the rational world of defense intellectuals. *Signs, 12*(4), 687–718. https://doi.org/10.1086/494362

Craig, R., Amernic, J., & Tourish, D. (2014). Perverse audit culture and accountability of the modern public university. *Financial Accountability & Management, 30*(1), 1–24. https://doi.org/10.1111/faam.12025

Dewinter, J., Kocurek, C. A., & Nichols, R. (2014). Taylorism 2.0: Gamification, scientific management and capitalist appropriation of play. *Journal of Gaming & Virtual Worlds, 6*(2), 109–127. https://doi.org/10.1386/jgvw.6.2.109_1

Easterling, K. (2016). *Extrastatecraft: The power of infrastructure space.* Verso.

Elkin-Koren, N., & Haber, E. (2016). Governance by proxy: Cyber challenges to civil liberties. *Brooklyn Law Review, 82*(105–162).

Fisher, M. (2009). *Capitalist realism: Is there no alternative?* Zero Books.

Forsberg, E.-M. (2012). Standardisation in the field of nanotechnology: Some issues of legitimacy. *Science and Engineering Ethics, 18,* 719–739. https://doi.org/10.1007/s11948-011-9268-0

Glover, J. (2013). Digital taylorism: Hybrid knowledge professionals in the UK ICT sector. In C. Evans & L. Holmes (Eds.), *Re-tayloring management: Scientific management a century on.* Farnham.

Graz, J.-C. (2018). Global corporations and the governance of standards. In A. Nölke & C. May (Eds.), *Handbook of the international political economy of the corporation* (pp. 448–461). Edward Elgar. https://doi.org/10.4337/978 1785362538.00037

Hansen, H. K., Salskov-Iversen, D., & Biselev, S. (2002). Discursive globalization: Transnational discourse communities and New Public Management. In M. Ougaard & R. Higgott (Eds.), *Towards a global polity* (pp. 107–124). Routledge.

Hong, S.-h. (2020). *Technologies of Speculation: The limits of knowledge in a data-driven society*. New York University Press. https://doi.org/10.18574/nyu/9781479860234.001.0001

Kaufmann, M., Egbert, S., & Leese, M. (2018). Predictive policing and the politics of patters. *The British Journal of Criminology*, 1–19. https://doi.org/10.1093/bjc/azy060

Louis, M., & Maertens, L. (2021). Why international organizations hate politics: Depoliticizing the world. *Routledge*. https://doi.org/10.4324/978042946 6984

Marcuse, H. (1964). *One-dimensional man: Studies in the ideology of advanced industrial society*. Beacon Press.

McCulloch, J., & Wilson, D. (2016). Pre-crime: Pre-emption, precaution and the future. *Routledge*. https://doi.org/10.4324/9781315769714

Merry, S. E. (2011). Measuring the world: Indicators, human rights, and global governance. *Current Anthropology, 52*, S83–S95. https://doi.org/10.1086/657241

Merry, S. E. (2020). The problem of compliance and the turn to quantification. In M.-C. Foblets, M. Goodale, M. Sapignoli, & O. Zenker (Eds.), *The Oxford handbook of law and anthropology*. Oxford University Press. https://doi.org/10.1093/oxfordhb/9780198840534.013.43

Nieto Martín, A. (2022). *Global criminal law: Postnational criminal justice in the twenty-first century*. Palgrave Macmillan. https://doi.org/10.1007/978-3-030-84831-6

Pol, R. F. (2020). Anti-money laundering: The world's least effective policy experiment? Together, we can fix it. *Policy Design and Practice, 3*(1), 73–94. https://doi.org/10.1080/25741292.2020.1725366

Postman, N. (1993). *Technopoly: The surrender of culture to technology*. Vintage Books.

Powers, S. M., & Jablonski, M. (2015). The real cyber war: The political economy of internet freedom. *University of Chicago Press*. https://doi.org/10.5406/illinois/9780252039126.001.0001

Rosa, H. (2021). *The uncontrolability of the world*. Polity.

Sataøen, H. L. (2018). Regulokratene: Den nye styringsprofesjonen?. *Norsk sosi-ologisk tidsskrift, 2*(6), 481–499. https://doi.org/10.18261/issn.2535-2512-2018-06-03

Shenhav, Y. (2007). *Manufacturing rationality: The engineering foundations of the managerial revolution.* Oxford University Press.

Supiot, A. (2017). *Governance by numbers: The making of a legal model of allegiance.* Bloomsbury.

Taylor, F. W. (1919). *The principles of scientific management.* Harper & Brothers Publishers.

Tilahun, N. (2021). The re-organization of the FATF as an international legal person and the promises and limits to accountability. In A. Arcuri & F. Coman-Kund (Eds.), *Technocracy and the law: Accountability, governance and expertise* (pp. 131–154). Routledge. https://doi.org/10.4324/978100317 4769-6

Verhage, A. (2011). The anti money laundering complex and the compliance industry. *Routledge.* https://doi.org/10.4324/9780203828489

Williams, J. W. (2014). The private eyes of corporate culture: The forensic accounting and corporate investigation industry and the production of corporate financial security. In K. Walby & R. K. Lippert (Eds.), *Corporate security in the 21st century: Theory and practice in international perspective* (pp. 56–77). Palgrave Macmillan. https://doi.org/10.1057/978113734 6070_4

Woodiwiss, M. (2005). *Gangster capitalism: The United States and the global rise of organized crime.* Constable.

Yates, J., & Murphy, C. N. (2019). *Engineering rules: Global standard setting since 1880.* John Hopkins University Press.

Ylönen, M., & Kuusela, H. (2019). Consultocracy and its discontents: A critical typology and a call for a research agenda. *Governance, 32,* 241–258. https://doi.org/10.1111/gove.12369

CHAPTER 7

Artificial Intelligence, Algorithmic Governance, and the Manufacturing of Suspicion and Risk

Abstract We turn to the ways in which securitized and criminalized compliance is being built into the hostile algorithmic architectures that increasingly seek to govern our lives, and pre-empt crimes and harms, in the process turning workers, clients, suppliers, customers and others, into suspects, possible threats and risks to be continually monitored, surveilled, and managed. We return this gaze and discuss the suspect AI, the bogus promises, the flawed theories—albeit with real consequences. We think about ways in which the compliance-industrial complex and RegTech hybridize and expand the logic of intelligence, and the ways in which the operating system of a pre-crime society, being built as we speak by the compliance-industrial complex, is to be understood as a peculiar merger of surveillance capitalism and regulatory capitalism.

Keywords Algorithmic governance · Artificial intelligence (AI) · RegTech · Surveillance capitalism · Regulatory capitalism

The fetishization of risk assessments, of data-driven and evidence-based solutions, of quantification and other technobureaucratic instruments conveniently evades both moral and political discussion by cultivating a simulacrum of objectivity. But we rarely get to question the ways in which risks are *evaluated*, what measures are viewed as appropriate in the light

© The Author(s), under exclusive license to Springer Nature
Switzerland AG 2022
T. Ø. Kuldova, *Compliance-Industrial Complex*,
https://doi.org/10.1007/978-3-031-19224-1_7

of these risks and so forth. Once delegated to risk experts, the issues that once created moral outrage are depoliticized. As Mary Douglas and Aaron Wildavsky have nicely shown, 'there is a delusion that assigning probabilities is a value-free exercise. Far from being objective, the figures about probabilities that are put into calculation reflect the assigner's confidence that the events are likely to occur' (Douglas & Wildavsky, 1983, p. 71). Moreover,

> specialized risk assessment impoverishes the statement of a human problem by taking it out of context. The notion of risk is an extraordinarily constructed idea, essentially decontextualized and desocialized. Thinking about how to choose between risks, subjective values must take priority. It is a travesty of rational thought to pretend that it is best to take value-free decisions in matters of life and death. (...) Science and risk assessment cannot tell us what we need to know about threats of danger since they explicitly try to exclude moral ideas about good life. Where responsibility starts, they stop. (Douglas & Wildavsky, 1983, pp. 73–81)

For anyone who has conducted a risk assessment, be it as part of suspicious activity reporting or the now obligatory risk assessments of research projects, and who has assigned colour codes and numbers to all thinkable scenarios (and to scenarios manufactured purely to satisfy the demands of the risk assessment), this comes as no surprise. Any risk assessment involves a series of subjective and discretionary judgements. Suspicion also tends to quickly generate more suspicion. The more one digs into a case or a person, the more a suspicion can fester as new information becomes seen in the light of the suspicion. This goes also for the so-called data-driven assessments, even here the numerical values the assessments deliver are speculative. But these assessments and numbers acquire a reality of their own, presented as disinterested and neutral (and—the fallacy of it, *therefore* right). The same goes for all the rankings and indicators, on which many of these risk assessments rely, which are deemed objective—and therefore right. This is a grave misunderstanding of the very concept of objectivity. As Douglas and Wildavsky remarked already in 1983,

> Something has gone badly wrong with the idea of objectivity. It is taken out of context and turned into an absolute value for all discourse. The rules that produce objectivity rule out someone's subjectivity. In a context of justice, an objective judgment is disinterested (but not necessarily right). In a context of social inquiry, an objective report is honest, free of personal

bias (but not necessarily right). In a context of scientific inquiry, an objective statement is arrived at by standardized techniques; the inquiry can be replicated and under the same standardized conditions will reproduce the same answers. However objective the process, the interpretation is not guaranteed by the objectivity in research design (Douglas & Wildavsky, 1983, p. 73)

Despite this rather obvious insight, objectivity is being more and more often equated with truth and justice. As long as a pre-determined process was followed, we are being convinced to think that either truth or justice will automatically follow. This overestimation of objectivity is mirrored directly in the realm of governance, with its overreliance of the aforementioned expertise; the same way that subjectivity is being disavowed, and supressed, the same way politics, too, is being disavowed and supressed. Or as Sally Eagle Merry put it,

> the expansion of the use of indicators in global governance means that political struggles over what human rights mean and what constitutes compliance are increasingly transformed into technical questions of measurement, criteria, and data accessibility (...) the legal process of judging and evaluating is transformed into a technical issue of measurement and counting by the diligent work of experts. (Merry, 2020, p. 243)

These numbers are sold to us as 'hard' supports for decision-making; automation, big data analytics, and statistical modelling combined with expertise not only obscure the subjectivities involved but also actively seek to eliminate them. Where the human is positioned as fallible, biased, emotional, and so forth, technological systems step in with their image of rational cool, cultivating the illusion of objectivity and neutrality. The compliance-industrial complex is precisely in the business of delivering this speculative expertise cloaked in objectivity, it delivers 'intelligence' (which too is always already uncertain), risk-scores, and other forms of quantified uncertainty that promise to combat and control the uncertainty of possible risky futures, while smoothly weaving security, surveillance, and private intelligence services into its fold. There are thus providers such as Prewave, which promise to deliver supply chain risk intelligence and compliance and sustainability solutions using their AI-powered intelligence-generating platform.[1] It promises to predict and anticipate a broad spectre of risks: from legal stress, cyber risks, natural disasters, product incidents, operational risks, governance risks, compliance risks, political unrest, financial stress, CSR incidents, consumer unrest, to labour unrest (Grill, 2021). Prewave, for instance, claims to have predicted strikes across major seaports in 2017 in Indonesia two weeks in advance, by detecting 'consistent pre-signals in social media', delivering a 'high risk event prediction of mass strike with a date and location'.[2] These technologies are sold in the name of supply chain due diligence, a growing area of compliance, especially following the German Supply Chain Law (*Lieferkettengesetz*) coming into force in 2023, aimed to hold companies with more than 3000 employees accountable for human rights violations in their supply chains, imposing an obligation to detect these through due diligence. The manufacturing of data and risk assessments in the name of transparency thus becomes imperative in order to be seen as compliant and have a proof on file, protect their reputations, and maybe even manage to supress a strike here and there; activists like to call it openwashing.

ON THE (SUSPECT) PROMISES OF ARTIFICIAL INTELLIGENCE

Edward Snowden once remarked that 'the greatest danger still lies ahead, with the refinement of artificial intelligence capabilities, such as facial and pattern recognition. An AI-equipped surveillance camera would be not merely be a recording device but could be made into something closer to an automated police officer'.[3] Given that AI is increasingly marketed as the key to much of future compliance solutions, as well as to intelligence-led policing and security practices—or even erasing the distinctions between these as they are predicated on the same epistemologies of probability, risk and prediction (Amoore, 2013), it is worth taking a closer look at the promises sold in its name on the intertwined markets

---

[1] https://www.prewave.com/ (last accessed August 20, 2022).

[2] https://f.hubspotusercontent30.net/hubfs/8402685/Case%20Studies/Prewave_C ase_Study_Seaport_Closures.pdf (last accessed August 20, 2022).

[3] https://www.theguardian.com/us-news/ng-interactive/2019/sep/13/edward-sno wden-interview-whistleblowing-russia-ai-permanent-record.

for compliance, security, and risk management. We can, for instance, read that:

> Anheuser-Busch, the largest brewing company in the United States, is once such company that is using an AI system to meet compliance standards. As Kimberly Pack, associate general counsel of compliance for Anheuser-Busch, described it: "One of the things that we're super proud of is our proprietary AI data analyst system BrewRight. We use that data for Foreign Corrupt Practices Act compliance. We use it for investigations management. We use it for alcohol beverage law compliance."
>
> She also pointed out that the BrewRight AI system is useful for discovering internal malfeasance as well. "Just general employee credit card abuse. ... We can even identify those kinds of things," Pack said. "We're actively looking for outlier behavior, strange patterns or new activity. As companies we have this data, and so the question is how are we using it, and artificial intelligence is a great way for us to start being able to identify and mitigate some risks that we have."[4]

Artificial intelligence (AI) is increasingly viewed as *the* technology of the future that will radically transform the world that we live in (Mayer-Schönberger & Cukier, 2013). If trained on large data sets, predictive algorithms are said to become capable of delivering *expert intelligence* within milliseconds, outperforming the professional judgement, and discretion of the best experts (Bullock, 2019). The rise of big data, driven by transnational tech giants—Google, Microsoft, Amazon, IBM, Meta, and so on, has led to the boom of machine learning, which, not unlike their financial capital, is swallowing ever new areas of life and reshaping the way we interact with, perceive and act in the world, often in opaque ways. Tech-optimists across the private and public sectors envision artificial intelligence to rapidly revolutionize all areas of life: from trade, consumption, services, communication, health care, criminal justice, welfare, environment, cities, traffic, work, and love, to the ways in which we wage wars, protect our safety, and police societies. Artificial intelligence promises to deliver cost-effective solutions, increase productivity and profit, streamline workflow, and thus free up human creativity—a promise that is eternally postponed. Its promise is one of a neoliberal data-driven technocratic market rationality of profit, efficiency,

---

[4] https://ccbjournal.com/articles/new-rules-new-tools-ai-and-compliance (last accessed August 20, 2022).

evidence, cost-effectiveness, 'best practice' and 'objectivity'. This logic threatens to erase privacy and the public sphere, as much as human discretion and politics proper, commodifying any bit of data in its way. It relies on surveillance of each and every minute detail of our everyday mundane activities, on us trusting our personal data to corporate platforms, on us using personal data as currency to pay for their services. Reckless data mining is the new gold rush, fuelling both inequality and injustice (Noble, 2018; Valentine, 2019). 'The age of surveillance capitalism' (Zuboff, 2019) is driven by manufacturing of ever new ways of monetization of aggregated private data. One of the growing strategies of monetization of big data is the security business: the development of ever new tools for risk assessment and predictive analytics for both the private and public sector. Not only intelligence agencies, but also police departments across the globe are either already using or testing artificial intelligence to support decision-making, evaluate risk, or to directly attempt to replace human police work. The nature of professional discretion within the field of security and policing is being transformed by automated decision-making systems driven by visions of early identification of hostile intent that would enable pre-emptive deterrence (McCulloch & Wilson, 2016). It is precisely this trend that is being integrated into compliance.

Surveillance cameras that Snowden recently feared for, be they those augmented through deep-learning cloud-based solutions such as those developed by IC Realtime, or those with built-in artificial intelligence systems, such as the DNNCam™ developed by Boulder AI, are already being trained and used, promising to deliver real-time intelligence. Potential markets include not only the usual suspects—military, police, private security, and corporations— but also schools, hospitals, and universities. IC Realtime CEO Matt Sailor remarked that these cameras can easily recognize when kids are getting into trouble using real-time analytics and offer pre-emptive notifications for a fight; the system just has to be able to spot a pattern—students crowding and moving in certain ways—and alert a human.[5] Schools in the UK have already implemented classroom monitoring software, not least in response to the UK Counterterrorism and Security Act from 2015 and the idea of a pre-crime student is emerging where 'students might be punished for disciplinary offences, or even crimes that they have not committed' (Hope, 2021,

---

[5] https://www.theverge.com/2018/1/23/16907238/artificial-intelligence-surveillance-cameras-security (last accessed August 20, 2022).

p. 122). The lines between private and public surveillance are not only increasingly blurred, but the private surveillance technology companies supplying these products to the government 'wield an undue influence over public police today in ways that aren't widely acknowledged, but have enormous consequences for civil liberties and police oversight' (Joh, 2017b, p. 102). Police departments across the globe are increasingly embracing artificial intelligence to support decision-making, evaluate risk, or to directly replace human police work (Joh, 2017a); and we are told that there is no doubt that 'big data policing is the future of law enforcement' (Ferguson, 2018, p. 509). The New York police department, to take one example, is a great source of inspiration on matters of tech use in policing for police departments across the globe. A document published by the *Brennan Center for Justice* lists all the technologies currently used that are *publicly* known (the department insists on secrecy and not all technologies in use are known), these range from: facial recognition, video analytics, social media monitoring, criminal group database, predictive policing, cell site simulators, automated licence plate readers, domain awareness system, drones, X-ray vans, gunshot detection system (ShotSpotter), DNA database, body cameras, and SkyWatch and TerraHawk surveillance towers.[6]

At the same time, the private security industry is rapidly growing, in numbers and in influence on policing—public and private—worldwide (Diphoorn & Grassiani, 2018; Kuldova, 2020; Schreier & Caparini, 2005), driven by the techno-solutionist visions of the Silicon Valley (Morozov, 2013). As security becomes increasingly commodified and risk commercialized, partnerships between private security companies and law enforcement agencies, military, and secret services grow as well (Ben Jaffel & Larsson, 2022; den Boer, 2011). These partnerships are also increasingly intertwined with the compliance-industrial complex, as we have noted earlier, something that precisely constitutes it as a *transversal* phenomenon.

There is emerging scholarship that widely agrees that the adoption of these technologies and the tightening of the bonds between law enforcement agencies and private security tech and data analytics companies is already reshaping ways in which we police societies, organize police work, produce criminal intelligence, prevent crime and enforce pre-emptive

---

[6] https://www.brennancenter.org/sites/default/files/2019-10/2019_NewYorkPolicy Technology.pdf (last accessed August 20, 2022).

security measures, while impacting levels of societal trust and perceptions of legitimacy (e.g. Brayne, 2017; Egbert & Krasmann, 2019; Ferguson, 2017, 2018; Joh, 2016, 2017b; Kaufmann et al., 2018; McQuade, 2006; Tyler, 2011; Wilson, 2019). Policing is thus becoming ever more hybrid and rhizomatic as new players proliferate, and as technological companies embed behavioural nudges and law itself into the code (Susskind, 2018). As securitized and criminalized compliance increasingly embraces these technologies, it becomes even more visible that we are dealing with technologies of governance, first and foremost. Technologies that demand compliance, and where any form of resistance is to be pre-emptively targeted and eliminated. While these visions may not have as yet fully materialized, the market for these technologies and imaginaries alike is growing; it is clear that the pre-crime imaginary is perfectly aligned with the technocratic approaches to policy, with the logic of anti-policies, with risk management and the fetishization of expertise (even where it is dubious). And it is also clear that anti-policies via compliance almost naturally stimulate the implementation of such technologies, and the growth of these markets.

Compliance and monitoring software has experienced a massive boom during the COVID-19 pandemic, promising safety while delivering increased surveillance. Tools like the popular IBM Watson Works promised a safer and smarter return to work, but also increased the level of worker surveillance; IBM Worker Insights vouched to provide benefits such as the achievement of 'compliance with worksite plans, policies and procedures', the analysis of 'performance against targets', or increased 'compliance and productivity'[7]; among the techniques used: social distance monitoring through tracking of distance between employees, monitoring of biometric employee data for vital signs, elevated body temperature monitoring, face mask detection, and more. While these systems focus on the management of bodies, others are predicted to increasingly focus on the management of minds through the reading of the body and AI, utilizing the same logic of surveillance: the analysis of emotion through speech, voice, facial expressions, language, sentiment, and other traces of the body deemed as providing insight into its inner (well-)being. Companies such as Hume.ai already promise to

---

[7] https://www.ibm.com/downloads/cas/OMXBA5RA (last accessed August 20, 2022).

deliver 'world's most accurate and comprehensive tools for understanding nonverbal behavior':

> Human values lie beyond words: in tones of sarcasm, subtle facial movements, cringes of emphatic pain, laughter tinged with awkwardness, sighs of relief, and more. We can help you read between the lines.[8]

These promises can reveal themselves to be utterly bogus, such as in the case of Vibraimage,[9] which—despite being revealed as a suspect, at best (Wright, 2021)—keeps on selling its software, promising to detect and quantify mental and emotional states from vibrations captured on video footage, and to spot suspicious behaviours, aggression, negativity and even lies; the software has been purchased even by several governments and security agencies. Vibraimage even relies on manufacturing of dubious expertise, and pseudo-scientific legitimation or as Wright put it,

> Making Vibraimage's interpretation and knowledge of a subject's mental–emotional state more convincing and authoritative than that of the individual is accomplished through processes of quasi-scientific legitimation(articles, conferences), design (sleek data visualisations) and performance (testing procedure, appeals to the precision of AI, authoritative operator), combined with the corporate power of public and private security infrastructure and a lack of knowledge, awareness or will to intervene in a booming market among politicians and regulators. (Wright, 2021, p. 15)

Wright has accurately analysed this and similar technologies as 'suspect AI', one that, despite the bogus promises, holds increasing power, no less through the fetishization of data-driven prediction and through 'the ambiguity and opacity of the system's algorithmic knowledge production' through which 'the operator can determine – in both senses simultaneously – the emotions, character, current intentions and future behaviour of the subject' (Wright, 2021, p. 15). A similar case of suspect AI has been the iBorderCtrl project, despite being funded with 4,5 million EUR by Horizon 2020. iBorderCtrl promised to deliver, among others, a so-called automatic deception detection system, or an AI-driven 'lie detector', a

---

[8] https://hume.ai/products (last accessed August 20, 2022).

[9] https://www.psymaker.com/vibraimage/ (last accessed August 20, 2022).

virtual policeman avatar that interviews travellers through a pre-arrival screening video and looks for micro-gestures that would reveal potential signs of deception and thus *threats*, assigning a risk evaluation to individuals based on how well they do in the interview. The system has been rightly criticized for being pseudoscience[10] and for inevitably producing large numbers of false positives, while reproducing different forms of bias (Kuldova, 2020; Sánchez-Monedero & Dencik, 2022). While these examples of suspect AI are likely not unique, discussions about the use of these technologies in compliance are ongoing, while some of them are already being built into compliance software solutions, in the name of science, objectivity, and best practice.

Artificial intelligence is, with the help of a considerable PR machinery, not only being promoted as inherently good, but also 'naturalised as "common sense" and a "public good"' (Bourne, 2019, p. 109). It thus aligns well with anti-policies, with the quest for a pure, safe, and good world. In line with the logic of 'capitalism with a human face' (Žižek, 2009), artificial intelligence is sold as key to addressing the *UN Sustainable Development Goals* (SustainAbility, 2019), including the goal of secure, just and inclusive societies. Agenda-setting initiatives such as the *AI for Good Foundation* or the United Nations annual *AI for Good Global Summit* (est. 2017) formulate core principles of 'AI for good' that are increasingly embraced and implemented by government's worldwide (Moore, 2019). Not only corporations, but government's worldwide are implementing AI powered systems, often through new public–private partnerships. And while there is no denying that artificial intelligence may find positive applications, such as in medical research, its applications in security, anti-terrorism, urban policing, and military interventions are far more problematic. While these have received some critical attention, the use of these technologies in compliance, built on the same logic, has barely received any critical attention. Technology is neither neutral or objective, as this PR machinery would like to convince us, but deeply ideological; and in the case of artificial intelligence and machine learning—only as good as the data that it is fed.

The now notorious Chinese Social Credit System (SCS) is a case in point of *centralized state surveillance infrastructure* integrating data

---

[10] https://www.theguardian.com/world/2018/nov/02/eu-border-lie-detection-system-criticised-as-pseudoscience (last accessed August 21, 2022).

collection, mining, and analysis from across state databases, social media, cell phones, banks, and so on, and utilizing artificial intelligence driven predictive analytics. It aims to monitor the 'creditworthiness' and 'trustworthiness' of citizens, companies, and organizations, and govern them through a system of rewards and punishments, while controlling public opinion, managing individual behaviour, and enhancing law enforcement. While we may like to think the perverse consequences of 'algorithmic governance' (Kalpokas, 2019; Katzenbach & Ulbricht, 2019) and state surveillance away by virtue of relegating it to the trope of 'authoritarian China', we do not have to go as far as China to see the algorithmic governance, surveillance, and policing proliferate. The Snowden disclosures of the National Security Agency (NSA) in the United States have already shown us the combined power of big data, private tech companies, and intelligence agencies (Lyon, 2014). And, is not KYC, enhanced due diligence, insider threat management, workplace monitoring, and so on, already sorting workers, clients, suppliers, into trustworthy and untrustworthy, good and bad, low-risk and high-risk, generating intelligence dossiers on individuals, and companies alike?

'Trust hard data. Not hunches. Trust LineSight®'. This is the tagline of LineSight®, a threat assessment system used by US Customs and Border Patrol and developed by Unisys following the terrorist attacks in 2001. In the aftermath of 9/11, lack of cross-agency collaboration and data sharing has been flagged as the number one failure of the security establishment (Hocevar et al., 2006; Snowden, 2019). As a result, collaboration and information sharing across governmental agencies and across nations has not only been stimulated, but increasingly integrated with big data analysis of corporate data, bank data, social media, online traffic, biometric, and other personal data. Edward Snowden revealed the scale of this indiscriminate global *mass* surveillance of entire populations which also changed the very nature of intelligence—making it fundamentally data-driven. By now, we are all familiar with the mass surveillance programs of the NSA and CIA, as well as the covert large-scale surveillance programs in different EU member states—UK, Sweden, France, and Germany (Bigo et al., 2013). But big data and artificial intelligence are being embraced by the police and border control alike (Joh, 2016, 2017a). Practices previously reserved more or less to secret services and security agencies are becoming mainstream: intelligence-led policing is embraced by police departments across the globe and companies such as Palantir are at the forefront of developing artificial intelligence predictive tools for police departments across the globe—and: for private sector compliance. These international trends in security, intelligence, and policing are enabled by increasing levels of digitization, Internet of Things (IoT), and smart cities projects—as much as by our willingness to give away private data and embrace the logic of surveillance in our everyday lives: be it through self-monitoring, or submission to the logic of gamification—a playful form of surveillance that provides us with pleasure (Whitson, 2013).

LineSight™ by Unisys is just one product among many, belonging to a range of big data and artificial intelligence driven risk assessment and near real-time predictive tools delivered by private corporations to government agencies and private actors across the globe. It aggregates data from across government agencies, banks, corporations, and online platforms to deliver a mathematical risk evaluation of passengers *before* they board a flight, promising to flag threats, and suspects before the threat they pose materializes.[11] From this market, LineSight™ has expanded in the context of the COVID-19 pandemic, in a manner of function creep, into detection of 'fraud, waste and abuse in the Public Sector Benefits program',[12] which in many ways resembles the KYC and data-driven due diligence technologies on the market.

Data-driven predictions, risk assessments, and algorithmic decisions are sold by tech developers as 'evidence' and 'intelligence'—as something 'solid' in 'liquid times' (Bauman & Lyon, 2013), as the 'transparent truth', as 'pure', unspoiled by human emotion, prejudice, discretion, and judgement (Kuldova, 2020). But what counts as data and how it is collected, what is included and what excluded, and so on, reflects historical, representational, cultural, and other biases. Prejudices about criminality of certain groups can be built into crime data, resulting in strengthening of these prejudices and self-fulfilling prophecies in place of predictions (Marda & Narayan, 2020). Bias has been shown time and again as endemic to the criminal justice system (Paneyakh, 2014), and to the data-driven 'actuarial justice'; it does not disappear, or become mysteriously purified through the use of technology, to the contrary, we risk that it will be magnified, with profound consequences for human

[11] https://www.unisys.com/news-release/unisys-unveils-linesight-advanced-analytics-based-solution/ (last accessed August 21, 2022).

[12] https://patechcon.harrisburgu.edu/wp-content/uploads/2020/08/Track-4-Unisys_LinesightFraudWasteAndAbuse.pdf (last accessed August 21, 2022).

rights and privacy (Cohen, 2013; Murphy, 2017; Risse, 2019). There is a growing critical scholarship pointing to the unintended harms related to the use of these technologies (Benjamin, 2019); we read about the inevitable problems associated with systems trained on biased and 'dirty' data (Valentine, 2019), about 'rogue algorithms' (O'Neil, 2016), 'algorithmic injustice' (Mbadiwe, 2018), 'algorithms of oppression' (Noble, 2018), and 'sexist and racist AI' (Zou & Schiebinger, 2018). Algorithms can reinforce existing racist biases and inequalities, creating 'a pernicious feedback loop', where 'policing itself spawns new data, which justifies more policing' (O'Neil, 2016, p. 87) resulting in an algorithmic self-fulfilling statistical prophecy rather than 'prediction' (Brayne, 2017), further criminalizing already marginalized people. The proliferation of algorithmic injustice can also trigger a deeper crisis of legitimacy, as 'new rhizomatic structures in the policing field' emerge, and 'the fuzziness of task distributions between different stakeholders, and concerns of accountability and transparency' (Nagy & Kerezsi, 2020, p. 20) become more acute. In the United States, citizens have been mobilizing to challenge the opaque predictive policing systems that target and harm them, questioning their accuracy, accountability and transparency.

While great hopes are invested in political and corporate visions of AI for social good, simultaneously, we are seeing a rise of critical voices that point to the unintended social and individual harms related to the use of these technologies (Benjamin, 2019). Predictive policing tools, such as the notorious PredPol, have been time and again shown to be little more than dirty statistics put into a system—a technology that results in algorithmic reinforcement of racist biases and existing inequalities. Predictive policing software like PredPol 'create a pernicious feedback loop' under the guise of objective intelligence and evidence-led analysis where 'policing itself spawns new data, which justifies more policing' (O'Neil, 2016, p. 87). The result is an algorithmic self-fulfilling statistical prophecy rather than 'prediction' (Brayne, 2017). Moreover, this so-called prediction often further criminalizes already marginalized people and exaggerates existing inequalities (Ferguson, 2017; Fyfe et al., 2018; Kaufmann et al., 2018; Ratcliffe, 2016; Wilson, 2019). Fighting the large-scale implementation of these technologies is becoming increasingly difficult, if not impossible. PredPol is just one of many tools developed by Palantir Technologies, a company founded by the venture capitalist Peter Thiel (also a founder of PayPal), who served as Trumps advisor, heavily supported his campaign, and who used to serve on the board of Facebook. Palantir is one of the most prominent software companies specializing in big data analytics and developing solutions for Pentagon, CIA, NSA, FBI, defence, intelligence, and security industries. Another Palantir predictive policing tool used by the Los Angeles police, LASER (*Los Angeles Strategic Extraction and Restoration*) has been discontinued under the pressure of privacy and civil rights groups that deemed it racially biased and intrusive; the audit found not only that inconsistent data were fed into the system, but that the system as such that lacked oversight.[13] This is how the technology was described:

> The basic premise is to target with laser-like precision the violent repeat offenders and gang members who commit crimes in the specific target areas. The program is analogous to laser surgery, where a trained medical doctor uses modern technology to remove tumors or improve eyesight. First, the area is carefully diagnosed: Who are the offenders, and where and when are they involved in criminal activity? Plans are then developed to remove offenders from an area with minimal invasiveness and minimal harm to the people and areas around them. Extraction of offenders takes place in a 'non-invasive' manner (no task forces or saturation patrol activities), and the result produces less disruption in neighborhoods. Continuing with the medical analogy, by extracting offenders surgically, recovery time of the neighborhood is faster.[14]

The rhetoric of the extraction of a diseased and unwanted social element is nothing but a revival of a directly fascist rhetoric—at this point we should remind ourselves of the history of IBM and Nazi Germany, where the IMB punch card technology and tabulating machines, anticipating the rise of 'big data' and enabling detailed census, management and statistical analysis, provided similar 'surgical tools' to the Nazi regime (Black, 2011). Others have shown how the rise of 'physiognomic artificial intelligence' has revived the racist 'pseudosciences of physiognomy and phrenology' (Stark & Hutson, 2022, p. 922), claiming that it 'can purportedly predict whether an individual will commit a crime, a person's sexuality, if someone will be a good employee, a citizen's political leaning,

[13] 'LAPD ends another data-driven crime program touted to target violent offenders', *Los Angeles Times*, 12-04-2019, https://www.latimes.com/local/lanow/la-me-laser-lapd-crime-data-program-20190412-story.html

[14] The Los Angeles *Smart Policing Initiative*: Reducing Gun-Related Violence through Operation LASER https://www.bja.gov/Programs/LosAngelesSPI.pdf

and if a person is a psychopath, all based on external features such as the face, body, gait, and tone of voice' (Stark & Hutson, 2022, p. 928).

While LASER was discontinued under great pressure from the civil society, new tools are emerging and are being implemented with great enthusiasm. Palantir offers a range of products for compliance as well under the umbrella of Foundry, marketed as the 'operating system for the modern enterprise', including tools for financial compliance such as 360-degree Single Client View, while Palantir Gotham markets itself as 'the operating system for global decision making' for 'global defense agencies, the intelligence community, disaster relief organizations, and beyond'.[15] The widespread tendency to view technology, and AI in particular, as neutral, objective (emotionless), 'surgical' and free of bias is deeply problematic; 'raw data is an oxymoron' (Gitelman, 2013). Despite our knowledge of data bias and the resulting injustices and harms, tech solutions are sold using this very myth of neutrality and objectivity and the myth is embraced by powerful players—not only the companies selling these technologies, but also governmental agencies uncritically embracing the very same rhetoric—and even stimulating its use through anti-policies.

ON REGTECH AND ALGORITHMIC GOVERNANCE

The compliance-industrial complex can also be understood as a form of 'penal entrepreneurialism' (Freeley, 2016) which has emerged out the privatization and professionalization of security services and the 'dossier society' (Laudon, 1986). Not only do these actors extend the power of the state, but they also directly rely on the commodification and aggregation of public records generated by authorities, across the globe—be these utilized in sanction screening tools, background checks, enhanced due diligence or risk management tools. In other words, they scrape public data and sell these, in aggregated and searchable form, enhanced by data analytics and automated glossy visualizations, to both the public and private sector. Public criminal records and court data, as analysed in depth by Lageson, are harvested by the private background checking sector and informal 'people search' websites, and sold to anyone willing to pay—irrespective of the widespread inaccuracies in these dossiers and of the perpetual 'digital punishment', stigma, and harm (Lageson, 2020).

[15] https://www.palantir.com/platforms/gotham/ (last accessed August 20, 2022).

RegTech, the regulatory technologies industry—promising to cut the costs of compliance in a rapidly changing regulatory environment (such as is the case in the recent proliferation of sanctions screening tools), secure effective monitoring and surveillance of a broad spectre of threat actors, and deliver near real-time intelligence (Barberis et al., 2019)— relies on public records, typically in combination with OSINT, or else, on scraping social media, news sites and blogs for adverse media, and other sources to create dossiers on individuals and companies, or deliver near real-time intelligence on a diverse range of threat actors. The results, be it dossiers or risk scores, are deemed 'intelligence', and as such need not be accurate or proven beyond doubt: they are geared towards substantiation of suspicion and assessment of possible risk, towards speculation and uncertainty—one that always tends to privilege the potentiality of a threat scenario over its absence.

Criminal, threat, and risk labels can thus be assigned with impunity; dossiers can overflow with mistakes, mixed up identities, inaccurate information, dirty data, misleading visualizations, and more—not to mention being based on flawed theories or even pseudoscience; individuals and even organizations are deemed guilty until proven innocent—or preemptively eliminated. So long these products are deemed 'intelligence' to support decision-making, created in 'good faith', through 'best practice' and with the use of 'latest technologies'—which are often seductively marketed as 'military-grade'—there is nobody to be held accountable for the consequences. These algorithms and technologies are also proprietary, which means they are hard to scrutinize. But even if they were 'transparent' as many activists demand now, only few—again with expert knowledge—could make sense of these and even those experts are not guaranteed to ask the more principled questions. Would a (corporate) data scientist be called to evaluate *social* bias? Whose expertise should count? Do experts know best? Can expertise provide an answer to fundamental political and moral questions?

Instead, these technologies are deemed as *the* accountability tools that are mobilized in the fight against both crimes and moral failings—can one hold accountability tools accountable? The state has as we have seen, through its regulatory agencies and supervisory bodies, delegated 'precrime' policing powers and intelligence gathering (Arrigo & Sellers, 2021; Hansen, 2018; McCulloch & Wilson, 2016) to an increasingly diverse set of private actors, from consultancies to tech companies and experts within organizations. But these actors do not have the same powers, or the same access to intelligence or police databases. They thus work actively around these limitations, be it by collecting and analysing open-source data in new ways, or by conducting private investigations into fraud, corruption, money laundering and other financial crimes, often multi-jurisdictional and under the guise of internal control, where coercive measures and surveillance techniques are used for which regular financial intelligence units would have to seek formal permissions under mutual legal assistance regulations (Meerts, 2016, 2020). That is, while access to some data may be restricted for private actors, in other ways they may have more power to investigate—such as access to employees' computers, emails, and so on; not to mention that in most jurisdictions private investigations remain largely unregulated, as do the uses of predictive technologies.

As a consequence, the compliance-industrial complex and RegTech tend to hybridize intelligence and expand its scope. The absence of some data also stimulates other approaches, be it psychological profiling, emotional and semantic analysis to create a 360-degree view of *risk*, or new techniques of forensic accounting which are readily available to corporate private investigators. As Meerts put it: '

> the absence of formal investigative powers may have sparked the creativity of investigators to take a broader approach to investigations and use methods of investigations that may be regarded as more private in nature. (Meerts, 2016, p. 175)

RegTechs, much like the product portfolios of big consultancy and audit companies, after all cater to the challenges posed by the expanding and increasingly complex regulatory environments across jurisdictions, from hard to soft—to which the same actors contribute, as we have seen, such as through involvement in private standardization, and from which they profit (Diller, 2012). As such, they build solutions for an extremely broad range of (increasingly intertwined) regulatory demands, which follow the same logic of compliance reliant on risk management and reporting of suspicions to authorities. In the process, these actors jointly tend to erase and blur old professional and subject matter boundaries. The reality is hybridized, functionalities layered and integrated within the same system; 'breaking-up the silos' as the compliance professionals call it, is a pronounced goal.

In practice, this means that it no longer makes much sense to separate AML compliance from anti-corruption, from sanctions screening and

CFT, or even from the emerging ESG (Environmental, Social, Governance) agendas, which stretch into prevention of human rights and labour abuses and the increasingly proliferating climate regulations and environmental harms. ESG compliance and reporting is again not to be thought of as separate from anti-corruption and anti-bribery, as well as another host of crimes; to the contrary, we can, for instance, read of the importance of 'ESG anti-bribery profile' and of the 'heightened focus on anti-bribery and corruption considerations and risks in the governance segment of ESG' which 'could also have the result of improving ethics and anti-bribery compliance in companies and organizations.'[16] It is fair to say that the logic of the AML architectures, of internal policing and endless generation of 'suspicious activity reports', has spread to encompass ever new agendas that span ever new 'anti-policies' (Walters, 2008).

While the critique of these technologies has been largely limited to questions of bias, discrimination, or reproduction of historical injustice, the more fundamental questions of the power to set the very *parameters for governance*, or else, to determine what matters and what is to be ignored—what is to be made visible and what is to be pushed into invisibility (Flyverbom, 2019)—tend to be systematically evaded. The compliance platforms developed by RegTechs are in no sense neutral or apolitical. To the contrary, the normativity of computational algorithms and their capacity to define the limits of our actions and imagination needs to be understood as a particular form of governance (Bauman & Lyon, 2013)—namely, *algorithmic governance*—which codes the hegemonic knowledge and 'best practice' into the de facto operating system of compliance. Algorithmic governance is a mode of 'ordering, regulation and behaviour modification, as a form of management, of optimisation', a form of social control based on rules involving particularly complex computational epistemic procedures 'characterised by inscrutability, the inscription of values and interests, by efficiency and effectiveness, by power asymmetry' (Katzenbach & Ulbricht, 2019, p. 11).

The compliance-industrial complex and with it also RegTechs do not only insert themselves into governance of global crime by virtue of their lobbying and corporate power vis-à-vis national regulatory and supervisory agencies, by virtue of their production of expert knowledge, but also through the more invisible forms of 'regulatory creep' through

---

[16] https://www.troutman.com/images/content/2/9/295067/Sharie-A-Brown-ESG-and-Bribery-LexisNexis.pdf (last accessed April 21, 2022).

internal compliance regimes and algorithmic control architectures. The emergence of the parallel supervisory technologies or SupTech, catering to the needs of supervisory agencies to keep up (or to their fear of missing out) by moving towards data-driven supervision, further blurs these boundaries and has been described as a 'paradigm shift in the relationship between regulation and supervision' (Chirulli, 2021). RegTechs and SupTechs contribute to the shaping of the concrete parameters of regulation and governance of crime and security by building largely opaque algorithmic architectures of control and monitoring, translating, finetuning and optimizing governance into practice, while selling their technologies as 'neutral' and 'objective' because they are technological, or as the only possible to satisfy regulators. As such, they further enhance the hegemonic language of technocratic expertise put into the service of anti-policies. They manage to present these technologies of governance as neutral despite widespread critique and knowledge of the great amounts of interpretation and discretion that go into building these systems, despite their often 'black-boxed' nature (Pasquale, 2015), despite the uncanny connections of these industries to the unhinged exploitation of consumer data, location data, social media, AdTech—what even a recent report by Meta (formerly Facebook) labelled as 'cyber mercenaries' generating new threats[17] (it appears no longer even paradoxical that new threat actors are assigned the role of fighting the proliferating threats). Despite all this, RegTechs are typically considered a mere *tool* of effectivization in a globalized world of increasing regulatory complexity; their increasing and hybrid role in global crime governance has largely gone unnoticed. The fact that critical knowledge is unable to break the grip of these phantasmatic visions of techno-social engineering and pre-crime, only testifies to their ideological nature. They are being embraced despite better knowledge.

ON THE OPERATING SYSTEM OF A PRE-CRIME SOCIETY

Intelligence and data-driven predictive technologies are used in compliance to profile, rate and evaluate external threats, creating (semi-) automated dossiers on suppliers, clients, customers, assigning risk scores to these and generating dashboards, seductive visualizations, graphic

---

[17] https://about.fb.com/wp-content/uploads/2021/12/Threat-Report-on-the-Surveillance-for-Hire-Industry.pdf (last accessed March 30, 2022).

representations of social networks, imitating the aesthetics of police files. Sanction screening tools, such as Sayari,[18] allow one to not only screen sanctions lists and link these to different public registries, but also to play with visualizations, to connect the dots, to generate convincing graphic representations of networks of companies and individuals, linked together both by economic relations and suspicion. KYC providers regularly promise to deliver AI-powered continual monitoring, beyond simple ID checks and list screening, including for example 'global intelligence on political, criminal and reputational risks', or 'exclusive deep and dark web intelligence',[19] and so on. One is likely to find technological solutions of this kind for whichever compliance issue one may encounter. What they share is their reliance on intelligence and the logic of pre-crime, effectively building these into algorithmic architectures that govern society in often invisible ways. While the use of predictive policing by state law enforcement agencies keeps on raising eyebrows, occassionaly resulting in the discontinuation of at least some of these practices, the use of these technologies by the compliance-industrial complex tends to go on virtually unnoticed. The fact that these systems are implemented under both the legal and moral obligation to act against security and criminal threats makes them legitimate, but also opaque—as they appear and reappear under different names.

The same data-driven pre-crime logic is also applied to insider threats: the employees or individuals with access who can pose a threat to the organization, such as the possible whistleblowers. Given the expert knowledge cultivated by the compliance-industrial complex, of AML, of anti-fraud, of anti-corruption, embracing rational choice theories and insights from the psy-complex, the focus is directed at the individual, at the expense of structural, systemic, and sociological perspectives (Rajan, 2020). Hence, these architectures also *target* the individual level. It is becoming increasingly common to speak of compliance in terms of psychology, in terms of the 'inner work life' (Amabile & Kramer, 2007) of employees, of their perceptions, emotions, motivations. There is an increasing preoccupation with emotions, affects and unconscious biases as objects of management, control, and compliance.

---

[18] https://sayari.com/ (last accessed August 21, 2022).

[19] https://www.kyc3.com/products/ (last accessed August 21, 2022).

Compliance software manufacturers relying on natural language processing and insights from the psy-complex are thus promising to automatically detect and risk assess, spot, and stop, or even predict and thus control individuals and instances of harassment, 'counterproductive workplace behaviours' (which often include trade union organizing), ethical breaches, or even negativity, cybersecurity breaches, insider threats, signs of fraud, and more, all possibly leading up to (or being 'predictors' of) serious crimes.

When it comes to unconscious bias it is worth noting that one can be deemed guilty without obviously being conscious of having caused harm, an accusation is sufficient; 'the presumption of innocence in such cases is replaced by the impossibility of innocence (…) in which guilt is assumed even when it cannot be proven' (Raymen, forthcoming). As anti-corruption and compliance came to encompass ethics and integrity management, ethics itself has become a battlefield for the fight against crime and focus has been shifting from mere compliance as rule-following to compliance as governance which encompasses integrity and ethics management. Soft and hard management techniques of manufacturing consent and enforcing compliance are thus combined (Huberts & Hoekstra, 2016). However, the soft techniques immediately harden when integrated into the algorithmic and digital architectures of compliance software. Algorithmic compliance architectures rely on data extraction and analytics that makes only certain things visible, while hiding others, underpinned by certain forms of knowledge rather than others, pushing and nudging the users in certain directions, functioning as a form of regulation oriented towards influencing human behaviour, while embedding and often even enforcing the actual regulations and guidelines and the accompanied sanctions.

In practice, if not in theory, the focus in managerial discourse has shifted from creating happy and hence productive workers, to making sure that even the *unconscious* is aligned with corporate policies and values, compliant with all regulations, guidelines, and internal routines. Crime and fraud prevention is thus not only individualized but also to be internalized, one is to perceive the world and the Other through the lenses of risk and threat. The goals are nothing less than 'governing the soul', so well analysed by Nicolas Rose (Rose, 1999). This governance of the soul, however, takes a far more coercive form when data-driven technologies of criminalized and securitized compliance informed by the intelligence industry are introduced; be it predictive insider threat management systems that evaluate and analyse employee behaviours, emotions, affects, language, and actions in real-time and (semi-)automate judgement and punishment, or systems that turn the gaze outwards, calculating risk scores, delivering threat assessments and intelligence dossiers on individuals and companies, subjecting clients, partners, suppliers, consumers, and others to increasingly intrusive surveillance and profiling to fulfil compliance obligations, in the name of fighting crime and corruption.

This governance of the soul is thus increasingly shaped by technologies of data mining and predictive analytics, and by the logic of security, intelligence and crime fighting. The enlisting of compliance and data-driven governance into the execution and implementation of transnational crime governance, foreign policy, and national security interests has profound implications for how we are perceived, treated, and governed as citizens, customers, clients, suppliers, businesses, how we are sorted, profiled, evaluated, managed, risk-assessed, threat-assessed, and our behaviour, actions and emotions predicted. A zero-trust environment is being created, not only in digital terms, an environment of suspicion, control, and legalese, an environment of ever-proliferating internal and external threats that are to be assessed and managed preferably in real-time and in alignment with the ever-evolving and ever-expanding regulatory landscape.

Griffith has rightly observed that technologizing compliance has reinforced and strengthened compliance as internal policing and identified a conflict between this logic and programs that aim to create 'compliance culture', warning against the dangers of technologized compliance (Griffith, 2016). But rather than being in conflict, concerns with culture, ethics and integrity have become *subsumed* under the same logic, subjected to quantification and measurement (Rorie & van Rooij, 2022), effectively colonized by data-driven internal policing: (predictive) policing and intelligence techniques are applied to ethical breaches. The realm of values and morals—and thus moral regulation and governance (Hunt, 1999)— is subjected to algorithmic and predictive surveillance architectures, where even the tiniest of breaches of the proliferating ethical policies and guidelines are flagged as 'conduct risk'. Stifling of critical and free speech is a natural consequence as is the effective break-up of any worker and union resistance, which is in management literature already labelled as 'counterproductive workplace behaviour' (Kelloway et al., 2010). Workers are labelled as 'bandits' and 'deviants' if they happen to run late for a meeting or whisper in the ear of their neighbour during a meeting—in the logic of zero tolerance and broken windows theory, these minor breaches indicate risk of possibly more serious issues along the line (Kelling & Wilson, 1982; Newburn & Jones, 2007; Prieto et al., 2016).

The compliance architectures built around crime, threat, and risk succeed in creating formalized control and surveillance structures, legitimized by legal compliance and risk management, where everyone—from employees, customers, clients, to third parties—is by default deemed a potential threat, risk, and criminal (of course, except for the rule-makers and rule-enforcers, despite all the 'tone from the top' rhetoric) (Nelson, 2021). HR departments act as private detectives, conducting background checks with the help of the latest automated tools such as Veremark that promises a 'new world of background checking'[20]; they are even supervising insider threat management monitoring systems. In a report by Ernst and Young, titled *Managing Insider Threat: A Holistic Approach to Dealing with Risk from Within*, we can for instance read that '56% of respondents view employees as the second most likely source of an attack, closely following criminal syndicates (59%)' (p. 1) and that the solution indeed lies in a creation of an 'integrated insider threat program' relying on 'advanced forensic data analytics' that can 'detect insider threats' and deliver 'risk ranking' of employees, relying on a data-driven 'risk-ranking score system' that comprises a combination of 'anomaly detection through machine learning', 'linguistic analysis' and 'assessment of "indirect" indicators'.[21]

These data-driven internal threat management systems promising to detect and predict different forms of organizational betrayal by current or former employees—from espionage, intellectual property fraud, financial crimes, unauthorized trading, to whistleblowing—are becoming an increasingly common tool in organizations. Different data-driven products leveraging new advances in machine learning, big data analytics and natural language processing are already on the market. These insider threat management systems are also being integrated into human resource management, performance management and compliance systems. The rhetoric of 'insider threats' is directly imported to the private sector and into compliance from the intelligence agencies and courses such as the

---

[20] https://www.veremark.com/ (last accessed April 21, 2022).

[21] https://assets.ey.com/content/dam/ey-sites/ey-com/en_gl/topics/assurance/assurance-pdfs/EY-managing-insider-threat.pdf (last accessed April 4, 2022).

one offered by Center for Development of Security Excellence, titled 'Developing a Multidisciplinary Insider Threat Capability'.[22] The examples of insider threats given regularly at compliance webinars, in courses and training sessions are those of Robert Hanssen,[23] the notorious FBI double agent, and Aldrich Ames,[24] the CIA double agent, both of who spied for Soviet and Russian intelligence. These examples are quickly followed the more contemporary figures of Edward Snowden and Chelsea Manning, positioned here as the iconic 'insider threats'. The report by the Intelligence and National Security Alliance (INSA), titled *Assessing the Mind of the Malicious Insider: Using a Behavioral Model and Data Analytics to Improve Continuous Evaluation,* uses precisely the examples of Snowden and Manning, to show that if predictive technologies, behavioural models, psychological profiling, social media analysis, sentiment analysis, personality mapping, psycholinguistics, emotion detection and more, would have been used, on a continual basis, the threat could have been discovered prior to materializing.[25] As we can read in the report,

> Certain personality traits may predispose an employee to acts of espionage, theft, violence, or destruction. These traits may be reinforced by environmental and organizational stressors. Less severe counterproductive work behaviors commonly occur before the decision to initiate a major damaging act. Clustering these behaviors into families may help define an "early warning system" and improve understanding of how individual characteristics and environmental factors may mitigate or intensify concerning behaviors. (...) Defining the clusters and families of measurable behaviors enables the creation of continuous evaluative tools to focus more quickly and effectively on critical concerning actions.

RegTech and compliance software utilizes these insights from HUMINT (human intelligence) only to build these into the algorithmic architectures

[22] https://www.cdse.edu/Portals/124/Documents/student-guides/INT201-guide.pdf?ver=i6-9pVZKmCd_72AXK5QeFg%3D%3D (last accessed August 21, 2022).

[23] For more see: https://www.fbi.gov/history/famous-cases/robert-hanssen (last accessed August 21, 2022).

[24] For more see: https://www.fbi.gov/history/famous-cases/aldrich-ames (last accessed August 21, 2022).

[25] https://www.insaonline.org/wp-content/uploads/2017/04/INSA_WP_Mind_Insider_FIN.pdf (last accessed August 21, 2022).

of compliance and organizational management, and merge these with OSINT. In another research paper, directed at IT and HR professionals, we can read that 'most insider threat incidents are the consequences of human actions, such as mistakes, negligence, greed, or reckless behavior' and hence their prediction requires a combination of behavioural monitoring and technical monitoring, 'any negative change in the behavior of an insider should be a concern for management' (Elifoglu et al., 2018, p. 61).

> The FBI also admits the risk from the insider threat is not technical, it is people-related, suggesting a behavioral monitoring approach. Previous FBI efforts to predict the malicious behavior with statistical models and technical monitoring did not fare well. Because of complications in determining the human motives and behavior, the technical monitoring tools should be complemented with behavioral monitoring tools without violating the local regulations about privacy (Dark Reading, 2013). The discontent at the workplace seems to be one of the most significant motives for the intentional privilege misuse. Layoffs, demotions, pay cuts, delayed promotions, or other management practices deemed to be unfair, provide the necessary justification for privilege misuse by a disgruntled employee, retiree, or business partner. An employee who did not receive promotion or recognition may be tempted to misuse his or her privileges or knowledge to reach sensitive materials. Stealing and selling confidential information may be considered revenge by the disgruntled employee (Elifoglu et al., 2018, pp. 66–67)

The same logic is already built into the Microsoft Purview's Insider Risk compliance solution, which promises to 'minimize internal risks by enabling you to detect, investigate, and act on malicious and inadvertent activities in your organization' and to 'help your organization prevent, detect, and contain risks while prioritizing your organization values, culture, and user experience.'[26] We can also learn that:

> Insider risks are one of the top concerns of security and compliance professionals in the modern workplace. Industry studies have shown that insider risks are often associated with specific user events or activities. Protecting your organization against these risks can be challenging to identify and

[26] https://docs.microsoft.com/en-us/microsoft-365/compliance/insider-risk-management?view=o365-worldwide (last accessed August 21, 2022).

difficult to mitigate. Insider risks include vulnerabilities in a variety of areas and can cause major problems for your organization, ranging from the loss of intellectual property to workplace harassment, and more. (...) Microsoft 365 risk prevention features are designed and built-in to our insider risk products and solutions. These solutions work together and use advanced service and 3rd-party indicators to help you quickly identify, triage, and act on risk activity. Most solutions offer a comprehensive detection, alert, and remediation workflow for your data analysts and investigators to use to quickly act on and minimize these risks.[27]

The same platform is utilized for very different forms of risk and compliance issues—fraud, workplace harassment, IP theft, workplace violence, sensitive data leaks, security violations, conflict of interest, confidentiality violations, regulatory compliance violations, data spillage, policy violations, communication compliance breaches, use of inappropriate or discriminatory language, and so on[28]—testifying to the progressive integration of the risk and compliance universe into single governance platforms, which also provide not only alerts, but also pre-determined paths for remediation. The metaphor of compliance as the operating system of a pre-crime society gains another meaning here, as the hostile algorithmic architectures built around data-driven and intelligence-led suspicion become normalized, built into the everyday digital systems that workers across the globe use; and built in the name of compliance, security, protection and the good. The fact that these systems are predicated on the same logic as the predictive policing technologies that mobilize public outrage is rarely recognized. These technologies also smoothly integrate into different algorithmic management systems (Schildt, 2020) and platforms which tend to merge performance management with regulatory compliance and conduct risk and quality monitoring, as manifest in products such as Cognitive View.[29]

[27] https://docs.microsoft.com/en-us/microsoft-365/compliance/insider-risk-solution-overview?view=o365-worldwide (last accessed August 21, 2022).

[28] https://docs.microsoft.com/en-us/microsoft-365/compliance/communication-compliance?view=o365-worldwide (last accessed August 21, 2022).

[29] https://cognitiveview.com/pages/technology/ (last accessed August 21, 2022).

Other examples here are solutions such as those offered by Teramind[30] or NICE Actimize which offer a range of predictive surveillance technologies for compliance[31], identifying behavioural patterns of every employee, relying on sentiment analysis to deliver 'early warning systems' for potential misconduct and conduct scores for identifying conduct risk.[32] Or for instance RemoteDesk, which drew attention to itself when it marketed its software as the 'the most advanced AI-based Desktop Monitoring Solution and employee monitoring software for work-from-home *obedience*'[33] (emphasis mine). The company has since, rather tellingly, replaced the word obedience with 'compliance, productivity, and security'.[34]

RegTech technologies thus build partly on private data-driven financial policing and its modes of producing suspicion through the key ingredients of: '(a) a risk-based approach; (b) a theory of (ab)normality; and (c) a surveillance apparatus' (Amicelle & Iafolla, 2018), but tend to expand these architectures of control and suspicion into 360-degree control architectures that encompass anything from human resources, dynamic insider threat management systems to gamified hacks that promise to enforce cultures of compliance and integrity. They create not only a world of 'liquid surveillance' (Bauman & Lyon, 2013), but a world where this liquid surveillance both relies on and translates into increasingly hybrid forms of governance and management, where rules keep changing, risk indicators are added and tweaked, and where guilt rather than innocence is presumed—in the name of security, productivity, and compliance. Legal compliance as well as the striving for the ethical cultures of compliance effectively legitimize this 'function creep' and transformation of compliance into workplace surveillance for the purposes of (performance) management and labour control. They also provide the necessary

---

[30] The site offers live demo, which I recommend to the reader to have a look at to understand the logic of these systems better: https://www.teramind.co/ (last accessed May 5, 2022).

[31] https://www.niceactimize.com/compliance/holistic-surveillance.html (last accessed May 5, 2022).

[32] I recommend viewing this video by NICE Actimize, as it is representative of the logic of predictive compliance monitoring: https://vimeo.com/674503022/8852c8b17a (last accessed May 5, 2022).

[33] https://twitter.com/dhh/status/1366316233612816384 and mentioned here: https://www.theguardian.com/technology/2022/apr/27/remote-work-software-home-surveillance-computer-monitoring-pandemic (last accessed May 6, 2022).

[34] https://www.remotedesk.com/ (last accessed May 6, 2022).

legitimate interest for harvesting personal data and for intrusive surveillance—after all, only when using all this data can they prove that they have been compliant!

The ways, described throughout this essay, in which anti-policies and regulations have stimulated the growth of the compliance-industrial complex which is in turn reshaping the very forms of governance in its image—as securitized and criminalized compliance—while enlisting the latest technologies, have so far remained largely imperceptible to those studying AML, anti-corruption, and the global fight against financial crime from more policy-oriented perspectives. While the system may be deemed inefficient, as many have openly argued, in tackling the actual crimes, it can be argued that it is becoming indeed increasingly efficient in its secondary functions: in stimulating the growth of a transversal power apparatus that empowers the corporate sovereign.

But the various digital and RegTech platforms that control the internal control structures, may need to be audited and controlled soon, especially if they rely—as more and more do—on machine learning. The aforementioned concerns regarding unintended harms related to the use of machine learning, predictive technologies and data analytics (Benjamin, 2019), systems trained on biased and dirty data (Valentine, 2019), 'rogue algorithms' (O'Neil, 2016), 'algorithmic injustice' (Mbadiwe, 2018), 'algorithms of oppression' (Noble, 2018), privacy and rights violations, are stimulating—unsurprisingly—regulatory action. The failures of these systems, yet again, are generating new layers of techno-bureaucratic regulation, again, risk-based. In 2019, the *EU Ethics Guidelines for Trustworthy AI*[35] developed by the 'AI high-level expert group' were issued, wherein relevant stakeholders were urged to *voluntarily* commit to these guidelines, and implement relevant audit systems, transparency and data and privacy protection measures (Hickman & Petrin, 2021); these guidelines are neither binding nor backed by sanctions—they are yet another instance of 'soft law' (Abbott & Snidal, 2000; Jackson, 2010). Moreover, EU's AI Act is being anticipated, which will aim to nothing less than to 'set a worldwide standard, so much so that some refer to a race to regulate AI' and it will also 'create a process for self-certification and government oversight of many categories of high-risk AI systems, transparency

---

[35] https://ec.europa.eu/digital-single-market/en/news/ethics-guidelines-trustworthy-ai.

requirements for AI systems that interact with people, and attempt to ban a few "unacceptable" qualities of AI systems'.[36]

This anticipation has already managed to stimulate the algorithmic auditing business, projected to grow as the voluntary regulation will eventually be transformed into a directive or another form of harder regulation.[37] The algorithms of RegTech compliance solutions are thus to be audited in the future by third parties and risk-managed of course, especially when considered 'high-risk' algorithms, such as those profiling and risk assessing individuals; the result will be the risk management of technologies that profile and assign risk scores to individuals and companies through the very same notion of risk; the layering of control could not be more obvious as is the resulting obscurity of governance under the imperative of transparency. We should remind ourselves of the concise book by Buyng-Chul Han on *The Transparency Society* (Han, 2015), where he makes abundantly clear that a society of transparency is inevitably a society of control; monstrous one at that. There is indeed already certification for having been algorithm audited—performed by no other than ORCCA or O'Neil Risk Consulting & Algorithmic Auditing[38], a company whose CEO is Cathy O'Neil, cited just above, the prominent critic and author of *Weapons of Math Destruction* (O'Neil, 2016); the audited companies receive a nice seal and a certificate. And this is not to speak of the growing field of equally technocratic FinTech regulation facilitating private innovation and targeting micro-level issues rather than macro-level issues of power transfer to the private sector and the systematic undermining of public interest (Omarova, 2020).

The solutions that are being proposed are again typically limited to calls for *transparency*, accountability, *ethics*, oversight, fairness, intelligibility, elimination of bias (Ananny & Crawford, 2018; Ferguson, 2017, 2018; Kemper & Kolkman, 2018). Or else, solutions precisely in line with the logic of regulatory capitalism (Levi-Faur, 2017). The solutions to the unintended consequences of these technologies are equally technological and regulatory—merely an argument for *more* data to perfect the imperfect systems accompanied by endless pre-packaged ethics and audit

---

[36] https://www.brookings.edu/research/the-eu-ai-act-will-have-global-impact-but-a-limited-brussels-effect/ (last accessed August 21, 2022).

[37] As an example: https://idiro.com/algorithmic-auditing/ (last accessed April 22, 2022).

[38] https://orcaarisk.com/ (last accessed April 22, 2022).

reports providing a semblance of accountability. These solutions are ultimately pseudo-solutions that may lead to an increase of reporting, in line
with the rise of audit culture, but will hardly fundamentally transform the
practice itself (Shore & Wright, 2015). Similar calls for ethical, transparent
and explainable AI are emerging both from within computer science, law,
and social sciences (Cath, 2018; Hagras, 2018). A post-political discourse
of ethics has already come to dominate this emerging sphere of pseudo-
regulation, and a whole cottage industry focusing on the ethics of artificial
intelligence has emerged at the intersection of academia and private
sector, pushing the ideology of ethical AI. But ethics is not a political solution—as such it fits smoothly within the apolitical logic of technocracy.
It evades the fundamental questions, such as: should we outlaw the use
of facial recognition given the privacy rights violations, resulting harms,
and injustice? Instead, it asks: how can we do facial recognition *ethically*?
Ethics is perfectly integrated into the technocratic and technostrategic
language and as such does not allow breaking with it (Cohn, 1987).
It eliminates politics and disempowers critique, replacing it with expert
language, auditing, and impenetrable and vast amounts of regulations.
Ethical pseudo-solutions ignore and dismisses structural, organizational
and societal risks and harms, while suppressing any possibility for *principled* political regulation (Garsten & Jacobsson, 2011). This is the sign
of our times: principled political debate has become impossible vis-à-vis
the forces of capital, and vis-à-vis the forces of international rankings and
international organizations—be it IMF, UN, the World Bank, OECD or
EU. Despite the recognized 'challenges' and fundamental issues, governments do not want to miss out, to fall on diverse rankings that measure
levels of digitization, and so, they are more and more eager to collaborate
with the private sector and invest in artificial intelligence and other tech
for improved and more efficient public administration, smart cities, new
AI technologies for policing, and military intelligence. When competing
with other nations, there is no time to pause and think critically about the
impact of these technologies. All we can hope for, is more of the same.

References

Abbott, K. W., & Snidal, D. (2000). Hard and soft law in international governance. *International Organization, 54*(3), 421–456. https://doi.org/10.1162/002081800551280

Amabile, T. M., & Kramer, S. J. (2007). Inner work life: Understanding the subtext of business performance. *Harvard Business Review, May*. https://hbr.org/2007/05/inner-work-life-understanding-the-subtext-of-business-performance

Amicelle, A., & Iafolla, V. (2018). Suspicion-in-the-making: Surveillance and denunciation in financial policing *The British Journal of Criminology, 58*(4), 845–863. https://doi.org/10.1093/bjc/azx051

Amoore, L. (2013). *The politics of possibility: Risk and security beyond probability.* Duke University Press. https://doi.org/10.1515/9780822377269

Ananny, M., & Crawford, K. (2018). Seeing without knowing: Limitations of the transparency ideal and its application to algorithmic accountability. *New Media & Society, 20*(3), 973–989. https://doi.org/10.1177/1461444816676645

Arrigo, B., & Sellers, B. (Eds.). (2021). *The pre-crime society: Crime, culture and control in the ultramodern age.* Bristol University Press.

Barberis, J., Arner, D. W., & Buckley, R. P. (2019). *The regtech book: The financial technology handbook for investors, entrepreneurs and visionaries in regulation.* Willey & Sons Ltd. .

Bauman, Z., & Lyon, D. (2013). *Liquid surveillance: A conversation.* Polity.

Ben Jaffel, H., & Larsson, S. (2022). Introduction: What's the problem with intelligence studies? outlining a new research agenda on contemporary intelligence. In H. Ben Jaffel & S. Larsson (Eds.), *Problematising intelligence studies: Towards a new research agenda* (pp. 3–29). Routledge. https://doi.org/10.4324/9781003205463-2

Benjamin, R. (2019). *Race after technology: Abolitionist tools for the new jim code.* Polity Press. https://doi.org/10.1093/sf/soz162

Bigo, D., Carrera, S., Hernanz, N., Jeandesboz, J., Parkin, J., Ragazzi, F., & Scherrer, A. (2013). Mass surveillance of personal data by EU member states and its compatibility with EU law. *CEPS Paper in Liberty Adn Security in Europe, 61*, 1–65.

Black, E. (2011). *IBM and holocaust: The strategic alliance between Nazi Germany and America's most powerful corporation.* Dialog Press.

Bourne, C. (2019). AI cheerleaders: Public relations, neoliberalism and artificial intelligence. *Public Relations Inquiry, 8*(2), 109–125. https://doi.org/10.1177/2046147X19835250

Brayne, S. (2017). Big data surveillance: The case of policing. *American Sociological Review, 82*(5), 977–1008. https://doi.org/10.1177/0003122417725865

Bullock, J. B. (2019). Aritficial intelligence, discretion, and bureaucracy. *American Review of Public Administration, 49*(7), 751–761. https://doi.org/10.1177/0275074019856123

Cath, C. (2018). Governing artificial intelligence: ethical, legal and technical opportunities and challenges. *Philosophical Transactions of the Royal Society A, 376.* https://dx.doi.org/10.1098/rsta.2018.0080

Chirulli, P. (2021). FinTech, regtech and suptech: Institutional challenges to the supervisory architecture of the financial markets. In I. H.-Y. Chiu & G. Deipenbrock (Eds.), *Routledge Handbook of Financial Technology and Law* (pp. 447–464). Routledge. https://doi.org/10.4324/9780429325670-24

Cohen, J. E. (2013). What privacy is for. *Harvard Law Review, 126*(7), 1904–1933.

Cohn, C. (1987). Sex and death in the rational world of defense intellectuals. *Signs, 12*(4), 687–718. https://doi.org/10.1086/494362

den Boer, M. (2011). Technology-led policing in the European Union: An assessment. *Cashiers Politietstudies, 20,* 42–58.

Diller, J. M. (2012). Private standardization in public international lawmaking. *Michigan Journal of International Law, 33*(3), 481–536.

Diphoorn, T., & Grassiani, E. (Eds.). (2018). *Security blurs: The politics of plural security provision.* Routledge. https://doi.org/10.4324/9781351127387

Douglas, M., & Wildavsky, A. (1983). *Risk and culture: An essay on the selection of technological and environmental dangers.* University of California Press. https://doi.org/10.1525/9780520907393

Egbert, S., & Krasmann, S. (2019). Predictive policing: Not yet, but soon preemptive? *Policing and Society, 1–15.* https://doi.org/10.1080/10439463.2009.1611821

Elifoglu, I. H., Abel, I., & Tasseven, Ö. (2018). Minimizing insider threat risk with behavioral monitoring. *Review of Business: Interdisciplinary Journal on Risk and Society, 38*(2), 61–73.

Ferguson, A. G. (2017). *The rise of big data policing: Surveillance, race, and the future of law enforcement.* New York University Press. https://doi.org/10.2307/j.ctt1pwtb27

Ferguson, A. G. (2018). Illuminating black data policing. *Ohio State Journal of Criminal Law, 15,* 503–525.

Flyverbom, M. (2019). *The digital prism: Transparency and managed visibilities in a datafied world.* Cambridge University Press. https://doi.org/10.1017/9781316442692

Freeley, M. M. (2016). Entrepreneurs of punishment: How private contractors made and are making the modern criminal justice system—An account of convict transportation and electronic monitoring. *Justice, Law & Society, 17*(3), 1–30.

Fyfe, N., Gundhus, H., & Rønn, K. V. (Eds.). (2018). *Moral issues in intelligence-led policing*. Routledge. https://doi.org/10.4324/978131523 1259

Garsten, C., & Jacobsson, K. (2011). Transparency and legibility in international institutions: The UN global compact and post-political global ethics. *Social Anthropology, 19*(4), 378–393. https://doi.org/10.1111/j.1469-8676.2011. 00171.x

Gitelman, L. (Ed.). (2013). *"Raw data" is an oxymoron*. MIT Press. https://doi.org/10.7551/mitpress/9302.001.0001

Griffith, S. J. (2016). The question concerning technology in compliance. *Brooklyn Journal of Corporate Finance and Commercial Law, 11*, 25–38.

Grill, G. (2021). Future protest made risky: Examining social media based civil unrest prediction research and products. *Computer Supported Cooperative Work (CSCW), 30*, 811–839. https://doi.org/10.1007/s10606-021-09409-0

Hagras, H. (2018). Toward Human-understandable. *Explainable Artificial Intelligence Computer, 51*(9), 28–36. https://doi.org/10.1109/MC.2018.362 0965

Han, B.-C. (2015). *The transparency society*. Stanford University Press. https://doi.org/10.1515/9780804797511

Hansen, H. K. (2018). Policing corruption post- and pre-crime: Collective action and private authority in maritime industry. *Indiana Journal of Global Legal Studies, 25*(1), 131–156. https://doi.org/10.2979/indjglolegstu.25.1.0131

Hickman, E., & Petrin, M. (2021). Trustworthy AI and corporate governance: The EU's ethics guidelines for trustworthy artifcial intelligence from a company law perspective. *European Business Organization Law Review, 22*,. https://doi.org/10.1007/s40804-021-00224-0

Hocevar, S. P., Thomas, G. F., & Jansen, E. (2006). Building collaborative capacity: An innovative strategy for homeland security preparedness. In M. Beyerlein, S. Beyerlein, & F. Kennedy (Eds.), *Innovation through Collaboration (Advances in interdisciplinary studies of work teams, 12* (pp. 255–274). Emerald Group Publishing Limited. https://doi.org/10.1016/S1572-097 7(06)12010-5

Hope, A. (2021). Visions of the pre-criminal student: Reimagining school digital surveillance In B. A. Arrigo & B. G. Sellers (Eds.), *The pre-crime society: Crime, culture and control in the ultramodern age* (pp. 105–126). Bristol University Press. https://doi.org/10.1332/policypress/978152920 5251.003.0006

Huberts, L., & Hoekstra, A. (Eds.). (2016). *Integrity management in the public sector: The Dutch approach*. BIOS.

Hunt, A. (1999). *Governing morals: A social history of moral regulation*. Cambridge University Press.

Jackson, K. T. (2010). Global corporate governance: Soft law and reputational accountability. *Brooklyn Journal of International Law, 35*(1), 41–106.

Joh, E. E. (2016). The new surveillance discretion: Automated suspicion, big data, and policing. *Harvard Law & Policy Review, 10*, 15–43.

Joh, E. E. (2017a). Artificial intelligence and policing: First questions. *Seattle University Law Review, 41*, 1139–1144.

Joh, E. E. (2017b). The undue influence of surveillance technology companies on policing. *New York University Law Review, 92*(September), 101–130. https://doi.org/10.2139/ssrn.2924620

Kalpokas, I. (2019). *Algorithmic governance: Politics and law in the post-human era.* Palgrave Macmillan. https://doi.org/10.1007/978-3-030-31922-9

Katzenbach, C., & Ulbricht, L. (2019). Algorithmic governance. *Internet Policy Review, 8*(4), 1–18. https://doi.org/10.14763/2019.4.1424

Kaufmann, M., Egbert, S., & Leese, M. (2018). Predictive policing and the politics of patters. *The British Journal of Criminology*, 1–19. https://doi.org/10.1093/bjc/azy060

Kelling, G. L., & Wilson, J. Q. (1982). Broken windows: The police and neighborhood safety. *Atlantic Monthly, 249*(3), 29–38.

Kelloway, E. K., Francis, L., Prosser, M., & Cameron, J. E. (2010). Counterproductive work behavior as protest. *Human Resource Management Review, 20*, 18–25. https://doi.org/10.1016/j.hrmr.2009.03.014

Kemper, J., & Kolkman, D. (2018). Transparent to whom? No algorithmic accountability without critical audience. *Information, Communication & Society*, 1–17. https://doi.org/10.1080/1369118X.2018.1477967

Kuldova, T. Ø. (2020). Imposter paranoia in the age of intelligent surveillance: Policing outlaws, borders and undercover agents. *Journal of Extreme Anthropology, 4*(1), 45–73. https://doi.org/10.5617/jea.7813

Lageson, S. E. (2020). *Digital punishment: Privacy, stigma, and the harms of data-driven criminal justice.* Oxford University Press. https://doi.org/10.1093/oso/9780190872007.001.0001

Laudon, K. C. (1986). *Dossier society: Value choices in the design of national information systems.* Columbia University Press.

Levi-Faur, D. (2017). Regulatory capitalism. In P. Drahos (Ed.), *Regulatory theory: Foundation and applications*, (pp. 289–302). ANU Press. https://doi.org/10.22459/RT.02.2017.17

Lyon, D. (2014). Surveillance, snowden, and big data: Capacities, consequences, critique. *Big Data & Society, 1–13*, July-December. https://doi.org/10.1177/2053951714541861

Marda, V., & Narayan, S. (2020). Data in New Delhi's predictive policing system. *FAT* '20: Proceedings of the 2020 Conference on fairness, accountability, and transparency*, 317–324. https://doi.org/10.1145/3351095.3372865

Mayer-Schönberger, V., & Cukier, K. (2013). *Big data: A revolution that will transform how we live, work, and think*. Houghton Mifflin Harcourt.

Mbadiwe, T. (2018). Algorithmic injustice. *The New Atlantis: A Journal of Technology & Society, Winter*, 3–28.

McCulloch, J., & Wilson, D. (2016). *Pre-crime: Pre-emption, precaution and the future*. Routledge. https://doi.org/10.4324/9781315769714

McQuade, S. (2006). Technology-enabled Crime, policing and security. *The Journal of Technology Studies, 32*(1), 32–42. https://doi.org/10.21061/jots.v32i1.a.5

Meerts, C. (2016). A world apart? Private investigations in the corporate sector. *Erasmus Law Review, 4*, 162–176. https://doi.org/10.5553/ELR.000073

Meerts, C. (2020). Corporate investigations: Beyond notions of public-private relations. *Journal of Contemporary Criminal Justice, 36*(1), 86–100. https://doi.org/10.1177/1043986219890202

Merry, S. E. (2020). The problem of compliance and the turn to quantification. In M.-C. Foblets, M. Goodale, M. Sapignoli, & O. Zenker (Eds.), *The Oxford handbook of law and anthropology*. Oxford University Press. https://doi.org/10.1093/oxfordhb/9780198840534.013.43

Moore, J. (2019). AI for not bad. *Frontiers in Big Data, 2*, 1–7. https://doi.org/10.3389/fdata.2019.00032

Morozov, E. (2013). *To save everything*. Public Affairs.

Murphy, M. H. (2017, 2017/05/04). Algorithmic surveillance: The collection conundrum. *International Review of Law, Computers & Technology, 31*(2), 225–242. https://doi.org/10.1080/13600869.2017.1298497

Nagy, V., & Kerezsi, K. (2020). Introduction—Critical reflection in policing studies. In V. Nagy & K. Kerezsi (Eds.), *A critical approach to police science: New perspectives in post-transitional policing studies*. Eleven International Publishing.

Nelson, J. S. (2021). Compliance as management. In B. v. Rooij & D. D. Sokol (Eds.), *The Cambridge handbook of compliance* (pp. 104–122). Cambridge University Press. https://doi.org/10.1017/9781108759458.009

Newburn, T., & Jones, T. (2007). Symbolizing crime control: Reflections on zero tolerance. *Theoretical Criminology, 11*(2), 221–243. https://doi.org/10.1177/1362480607075849

Noble, S. U. (2018). *Algorithms of oppression: How search engines reinforce racism*. New York University Press. https://doi.org/10.2307/j.ctt1pwt9w5

O'Neil, C. (2016). *Weapons of math destruction: How big data increases inequality and threatens democracy*. Crown.

Omarova, S. T. (2020). *Dealing with Disruption: Emerging Approaches to Fintech Regulation Washington University Journal of Law & Policy, 61*, 25–54.

Paneyakh, E. (2014). Faking performance together: Systems of performance evaluation in Russian enforcement agencies and production of bias and privilege.

Post-Soviet Affairs, 30(2–3), 115–136. https://doi.org/10.1080/1060586X.2013.858525

Pasquale, F. (2015). The black box society: The secret algorithms that control money and information. *Harvard University Press.* https://doi.org/10.4159/harvard.9780674736061

Prieto, L. C., Norman, M. V., Phipps, S. T. A., & Chenault, E. B. S. (2016). Tackling micro-aggressions in organizations: A broken windows approach. *Journal of Ledership, Accountability and Ethics, 13*(3), 36–49.

Rajan, S. C. (2020). *A social theory of corruption: Notes from the Indian Subcontinent.* Harvard University Press.

Ratcliffe, J. H. (2016). *Intelligence-led policing.* Routledge. https://doi.org/10.4324/9781315717579

Raymen, T. (forthcoming). *The enigma of social harm.* Routledge.

Risse, M. (2019). Human rights and artificial intelligence: An urgently needed agenda. *Human Rights Quarterly, 41*(1), 1–16. https://doi.org/10.1353/hrq.2019.0000

Rorie, M., & van Rooij, B. (Eds.). (2022). *Measuring compliance: Assessing corporate crime and misconduct prevention.* Cambridge University Press. https://doi.org/10.1017/9781108770941

Rose, N. (1999). *Governing the soul: The shaping of the private self.* Free Association Books.

Sánchez-Monedero, J., & Dencik, L. (2022). The politics of deceptive borders: 'biomarkers of deceit' and the case of iBorderCtrl. *Information, Communication & Society, 25*(3), 413–430. https://doi.org/10.1080/1369118X.2020.1792530

Schildt, H. (2020). *The data imperative: How digitalization is reshaping management, organizing, and work.* Oxford University Press. https://doi.org/10.1093/oso/9780198840817.001.0001

Schreier, F., & Caparini, M. (2005). *Privatising security: Law, practice and governance of private military and security companies.* Geneva Centre for the Democratic Control of Armed Forces (DCAF) Occasional Paper No. 6.

Shore, C., & Wright, S. (2015). Audit culture revisited: Rankings, ratings, and the reassembling of society. *Current Anthropology, 56*(3), 421–444. https://doi.org/10.1086/681534

Snowden, E. (2019). *Permanent record.* Henry Holt and Company.

Stark, L., & Hutson, J. (2022). Physiognomic artificial intelligence. *Fordham Intellectual Property, Media and Entertainment Law Journal, 32*(4), 922–978.

Susskind, J. (2018). *Future politics: Living together in a world transformed by tech.* Oxford University Press.

SustainAbility. (2019). *AI & the sustainable development goals: The state of play.*

Tyler, T. R. (2011). Trust and legitimacy: Policing in the USA and Europe. *European Journal of Criminology, 8*(4), 254–266. https://doi.org/10.1177/1477370811411462

Valentine, S. (2019). Impoverished algorithms: Misguided governmnents, flawed technologies, and social control. *Fordham Urban Law Review, 46*(2), 364–427.

Walters, W. (2008). Anti-policy and anti-politics: Critical reflections on certain schemes to govern bad things. *European Journal of Cultural Studies, 11*(3), 267–288. https://doi.org/10.1177/1367549408091844

Whitson, J. R. (2013). Gaming the quantified self. *Surveillance & Society, 11*(1/2), 163–176. https://doi.org/10.24908/ss.v11i1/2.4454

Wilson, D. (2019). Platform policing and the real-time cop. *Surveillance & Society, 17*(1), 69–75. https://doi.org/10.24908/ss.v17i1/2.12958

Wright, J. (2021). Suspect AI: Vibraimage, emotion recognition technology and algorithmic opacity. *Science, Technology & Society, 1–20.* https://doi.org/10.1177/09717218211003411

Žižek, S. (2009). *First as tragedy.* Verso.

Zou, J., & Schiebinger, L. (2018). AI can be sexist and racist—it's time to make it fair. *Nature, 559*, 324–326. https://doi.org/10.1038/d41586-018-05707-8

Zuboff, S. (2019). *The age of surveillance capitalism: The fight for a human future at the new frontier of power.* Profile Books.

Epilogue

The Vicious Circle of Compliance and Defiance

The compliance-industrial complex builds on a peculiar form of control which relies on *imitation* and hybridization of the logic of the criminal justice system, intelligence, and policing—minus many of the guarantees of procedural fairness and due process of law. Architectures built in the name of fighting transnational crimes smoothly—in the manner of regulatory and function creep—transmorph into managerial control systems, performance management, employee surveillance and in promises to risk assess and profile any individuals, companies, clients, consumers, suppliers, anywhere in the world. The digital and algorithmic architectures of compliance software developed by RegTechs are not only turning regulations and law into code, but also creating new and more subtle forms of 'algorithmic governance' (Campbell-Verduyn et al., 2017; Kalpokas, 2019; Katzenbach & Ulbricht, 2019). What will be the consequences of the (semi-)automation of securitized and criminalized compliance as a preferred mode of governance, in the name of the 'good'?

At the same time as the formalized, juridified, and datafied architectures of the compliance-industrial complex come to prominence, we see that informal, professional, and cultural forms of social control with their informal sanctions and often unspoken but widely understood rules are eroding. Few are confident to rely on professional judgement and discretion, on shared morality, common decency. Instead, calls for formalized

T. Ø. Kuldova, *Compliance-Industrial Complex*, https://doi.org/10.1007/978-3-031-19224-1

and explicit rules and managerial 'compliance culture' with formalized sanctions, formalized procedures, and formalized processes proliferate. Audit, accountability, transparency, all demand submission and compliance with pre-determined rules and best practices. And indeed, this formalization generates a growing paper-trail and massive data-exhaust that serves as a *proof* of compliance. Suddenly, what cannot be reported is per definition deemed suspect; and what is on the paper tends to count for more than what is happening on the ground. What becomes more credible than reality, even if it points in a radically different direction, is having paperwork in place. Compliance platforms like Clausematch thus for instance specialize in data-driven control *of* compliance policies and of internal control systems, delivering 'clear evidence of compliance'[1] to the regulators, auditors, or stakeholders by supplying granular information and reports on when, by whom, each internal policy document and process has been amended, reviewed, approved, regulatory demand integrated, and revised guidelines distributed through the organization. That which is not captured is not only deemed suspect, but also often nonexistent; the fallacies resulting from the approach are obvious (e.g. the McNamara fallacy). But, interestingly, the layering of all these control apparatuses on top of each other does not seem to strike many as suspect. Since these control apparatuses appear to fail, time and again, is it not thinkable that they are part of the problem? Is it not plausible that they enable all sorts of moral evasions, that fraud and crime can easily disappear and vanish in these layered structures of control? Why is it that these forms of governance so uncannily tend to mirror the very logic of money laundering—adding layers of regulation, guidelines, standards, adding layers of complexity, proxies, and exploiting the possibilities of globalization?

The elimination of informality and its progressive equation with illegality is a larger social trend beyond the context of compliance (Nesvet, 2020). Informality itself is deemed suspect, both a possible sign or cause of corruption and of immorality itself, and hence something to be eliminated—this indeed reflects the developmental paradigm, the perceptions of the 'Third World' which shaped anti-corruption in its early days, and the quest to colonize the world through 'good governance', the fantasies of rule based orderand neoliberal reforms. The paradox may be that one

---

[1] https://www.clausematch.com/ (last accessed April 21, 2022).

now aims to create criminalized and formalized compliance 'cultures' to cover over the void of culture destroyed and expelled; in this sense, the very meaning of culture is being redefined as we speak. Another paradox is that informality appears to thrive at the top, while it is to be abolished downwards.

What has become abundantly clear by now is that the convergence of regulatory capitalism and surveillance capitalism—the exploitation of data combined with the delegation of intelligence and policing powers through the compliance architecture to corporations and other organizations—is creating a world of ubiquitous surveillance and hybrid governance, where boundaries are blurred, responsibility delegated and outsourced, layered, and accountability thus shuffled around. It also creates a world where the many are first and foremost viewed as suspect, as guilty until proven innocent—or rather even 'guilty until proven guilty' (Narayan, 2021), as threat, potential criminals, fraudsters, cheaters, or imposters (Kuldova, 2020). A world where that which does not conform to a norm, or a rule, to an average, everything that displays a deviant pattern of behaviour, is deemed suspect and threatening. And where the power to define what is deviant lies in the hands of the view, increasingly concentrated in the hands of the corporate sovereign.

These visions and fantasies of risk-based approaches and predictive intelligence-led decision-making are embraced by the industry and regulators alike. Both share the desire to break down silos, disrupt boundaries, and increase information sharing between public and private actors. They also share the underlying ideals of harmonization and integration through formalization, the vision of seamlessness now built into the algorithmic architectures. There appears to be no place one can go where this ideology has not taken hold, where it is not deemed the best practice, where it is not aspired to. Technological developments, the hype around AI, only accelerate the hybridization of compliance and its transformation from a remote, minor, and often disconnected legal department, which has often been viewed with suspicion, into a multidisciplinary governance function built into similarly all-encompassing algorithmic architectures. Or even, the operating system of a pre-crime society. The experts, too, regularly circulate across the imaginary boundaries of the public and private; many of those who have been around for a while have tried multiple hats in their careers, be it as professionals in regulatory agencies, supervisory authorities, law enforcement, financial and other intelligence services and other governmental bodies, and as compliance, AML, and financial and business intelligence professionals in the private sector, consultants in the Big Four and other audit and consultancy companies, or drivers of FinTech and RegTech. Alas, few dare to touch the obvious signs of what could be termed as corrupting 'influence markets' (Johnston, 2010) and revolving doors in financial crime regulation.

The expansion of the compliance-industrial complex has also stimulated the growth of what I like to call the *defiance industries*, or else the facilitators, intermediaries, and other agents of deception, often equally highly professionalized and with the same set of skills as the self-designated crime fighters, who are providing a broad range of services for layering of transactions, placement in offshore jurisdictions, obscuring of beneficial ownership, engaging in sanctions busting, and developing new modes of evasion while adding layers of complexity and opacity. Actors within the defiance industry considerably increase the difficulty of tracking and tracing organized crime networks, laundering of corrupt proceeds, structures of tax evasion, or sanctioned individuals and companies. This generates new threat scenarios and increases both costs of compliance and risks for companies, thus stimulating a market for their mitigation and for new, better, and updated data-driven analytics and intelligence products. This defiance industry, however, should not be imagined as somehow composed only of illicit or criminal actors. To the contrary, it appears largely well integrated into legitimate structures, often operating at the borders of legality and illegality, while highly skilled in the realm of the formalized and thus the more invisible. The realm of the 'lawful but awful', as one of my informants put it, is a realm of the formalized where structures of transparency can paradoxically serve as modes of generating opacity, obscurity, and secrecy. The role of audit companies and the Big Four in tax evasion schemes has been well documented (McBarnet, 1992; Sikka, 2016), as has been the role of evasion experts (Zucman, 2015). Or as one of my informants put it,

> The frauds that I have investigated, both big and large, where it has been assisted by a law firm, are innumerable. And people think lawyers are of high professional integrity. No, everyone I have ever come across would lie and cheat their way into millions of pounds and they would hide behind their own legality. ... In fact quite a lot of the crime and money laundering in the world would not exist without law firms and accountancy firms who were willing to go the extra mile on this. ... This is another reason why

I bailed out, if law firms do this, what can I say. There is a great line in the Godfather book, 'A lawyer with his briefcase can steal more than a hundred men with guns.' And it is 100% percent right, absolutely right, the major scale frauds and crime that is going on, is going on through law firms and accountants.

What would a critical criminologist answer in response to this essay on the compliance-industrial complex, on the pre-crime society that it is increasingly shaping, and on its simultaneous failures to prevent much of the elite crimes and frauds? Who is this complex designed to control? Dissent, critique, whistleblowers, workers? Whom is it protecting? The corporations, the governments and their security apparatuses? Whom is it empowering and whom is it disempowering? In direct opposition to the view of neoliberal ideologues of capitalism as fostering 'virtuous behaviour', critical criminology sees neoliberal capitalism as *criminogenic*, fostering the precise opposite; 'at its psychosocial core capitalism is little more than institutionalised insecurity, anxiety and envy in the service of a cold, abstract accountant's logic' (Hall & Antonopoulos, 2017, p. 121). Rather than virtue, is greed, fraud, and 'special liberty' revved up by competitive individualism, consumerism, managerialism, and the pursuit of shareholder profit at the heart of the economy (Hall & Wilson, 2014; Hall et al., 2012)? A question that a critical criminologist would thus ask is: does the system we have been led to believe is built to combat corruption, fraud, and more, in fact foster it while desperately trying to cover up its hollow core with layers of empty forms and empty ethics? Are we trapped in a vicious circle of compliance and defiance? A vicious circle where the one not only feeds the other, but the two also merge into each other? Where morality is hollowed out and the letter of the law twisted around against its spirit, reduced to a technical exercise best left to experts?

Many questions remain unanswered, and many of the subjects and dilemmas have been touched upon only in passing; much more could be said and investigated. But my hope is that this essay, following the spirit of a transversal and speculative inquiry spiced up with a dose of sociological imagination, has opened new ways of conceptualizing the phenomenon of compliance, freeing it from the technocratic discussions, and addressing it is a potent social phenomenon worth discussing, in academia and beyond.

References

Campbell-Verduyn, M., Goguen, M., & Porter, T. (2017). Big Data and algorithmic governance: The case of financial practices. *New Political Economy, 22*(2), 219–236. https://doi.org/10.1080/135 63467.2016.1216533

Hall, S., & Antonopoulos, G. (2017). Troika, austerity and the reluctant resort to criminality in Greece. In D. Whyte & J. Wiegratz (Eds.), *Neo-liberalism and the moral economy of fraud* (pp. 113–129). Routledge.

Hall, S., & Wilson, D. (2014). New foundations: Pseudo-pacification and special liberty as potential cornerstones for a multi-level theory of homicide and serial murder. *European Journal of Criminology, 11*(5), 635–655. https://doi.org/10.1177/147737 0814536831

Hall, S., Winlow, S., & Ancrum, C. (2012). *Criminal identities and consumer culture: Crime, exclusion and the new culture of narcissism.* Routledge. https://doi.org/10.4324/9781843925866

Johnston, M. (2010). *Syndromes of corruption: Wealth, power, and democracy.* Cambridge University Press.

Kalpokas, I. (2019). *Algorithmic governance: Politics and law in the post-human era.* Palgrave Macmillan. https://doi.org/10.1007/ 978-3-030-31922-9

Katzenbach, C., & Ulbricht, L. (2019). Algorithmic governance. *Internet Policy Review, 8*(4), 1–18. https://doi.org/10.14763/ 2019.4.1424

Kuldova, T. Ø. (2020). Imposter paranoia in the age of intelligent surveillance: Policing outlaws, borders and undercover agents. *Journal of Extreme Anthropology, 4*(1), 45–73. https://doi.org/10. 5617/jea.7813

McBarnet, D. (1992). Legitimate rackets: Tax evasion, tax avoidance, and the boundaries of legality. *The Journal of Human Justice, 3*(2), 56–74. https://doi.org/10.1007/BF02619290

Narayan, S. (2021). Guilty until proven guilty: Policing caste through preventive policing registers in India. *Journal of Extreme Anthropology, 5*(1), 111–129. https://doi.org/10.5617/jea.8797

Nesvet, M. (2020). Migrant workers, artisanal gold mining, and "more-than-human" sousveillance in South Africa's closed gold mines. In Y. Zabyelina & D. van Uhm (Eds.), *Illegal mining:*

Organized crime, corruption, and ecocide in a resource-scarce world (pp. 329–358). Palgrave Macmillan. https://doi.org/10.1007/978-3-030-46327-4_12

Sikka, P. (2016). Big four accounting firms: Addicted to tax avoidance. In J. Haslam & P. Sikka (Eds.), *Pioneers of critical accounting: A celebration of the life of Tony Lowe* (pp. 259–274). Palgrave Macmillan. https://doi.org/10.1057/978-1-137-54212-0_13

Zucman, G. (2015). *The hidden wealth of nations: The scourge of tax havens*. Chicago University Press. https://doi.org/10.7208/chicago/9780226245560.001.0001

INDEX

A

accountability, 4, 5, 15, 22, 25, 77, 109, 110, 127, 130, 143, 144, 154, 155

accounting, 5, 9, 10, 27, 37, 41, 49, 50, 56, 57, 60, 97, 98, 100, 101, 103, 131

algorithmic architecture, 5, 33, 34, 64, 78, 94, 103, 133, 134, 138, 140, 153, 155

algorithmic governance, 125, 132, 153

algorithmic injustice, 127

algorithm(s), 37, 119, 127, 130, 132, 143

anticipatory, 6, 36, 99

anticipatory governance, 5, 37

anti-corruption, 4, 5, 8, 9, 11, 23–33, 36, 38–40, 48, 60, 62, 74, 83, 84, 88, 91, 102, 105, 108, 131, 132, 134, 135, 142, 154

anti-policy, 6

anti-policy syndrome, 37, 38

anti-social behaviour, 82

apolitical, 104, 110, 132, 144

artificial intelligence (AI), 32, 41, 60, 90, 92, 108, 111, 117–127, 129, 134, 141–144, 155

auditing, 5, 56, 59, 65, 76, 87, 143, 144

audit society, 11

B

behaviour, 8, 25, 34, 60, 88, 89, 91, 92, 98, 100, 122, 123, 125, 132, 135, 136, 138, 141, 155

best practice, 6, 12, 22, 23, 25, 56, 62, 75, 84, 90, 101, 104–107, 109, 110, 120, 124, 130, 132, 154, 155

blurring, 35, 57, 76

bribery, 23, 28, 50, 52

C

capitalism, 7, 107, 157

code of conduct, 106

compliance, 5–16, 23, 25, 26, 28–36, 38, 40, 41, 48–56, 58–62, 64, 65, 74, 75, 78, 81–84, 87–93, 100–102, 105–110, 117–120, 122, 124, 126, 129–143, 153–157

compliance culture, 41, 51–53, 59, 136, 154

compliance-industrial complex, 10, 14, 21, 26–28, 32, 33, 35–41, 47–49, 51, 55, 59–62, 65, 66, 73, 76–78, 81, 86, 87, 90, 91, 94, 97, 100, 101, 104, 107, 108, 110, 117, 121, 129, 131, 132, 134, 142, 153, 156, 157

conduct, 5, 9, 10, 27, 34, 36, 38, 41, 51, 56, 58, 61, 65, 76, 77, 84, 93, 105, 106, 140, 141

consultocracy, 33, 47, 110

control, 5, 7–9, 12, 14–16, 27, 33, 34, 36–38, 48–51, 53, 55, 56, 58, 60–62, 64, 65, 77, 78, 90, 92, 103, 108–110, 117, 125, 131–137, 141–143, 153, 154, 157

corporate governance, 7, 54, 62

corporate power, 16, 31, 60, 132

corporate security, 55, 56, 60, 74, 75, 93, 103

corporate social responsibility (CSR), 7, 31, 58, 102, 118

corporate sovereign, 12, 15, 31, 58–60, 73, 83, 90, 142, 155

corruption, 3–5, 7, 8, 22–26, 28–39, 49, 50, 56, 60, 64, 65, 74, 82, 83, 86, 88, 103, 104, 106–108, 131, 132, 136, 154, 157

counterproductive workplace behaviour, 82, 135, 136

counter-terrorism, 10

crime, 5–9, 11–13, 16, 22–27, 29, 30, 32–36, 39, 47, 48, 52, 55–57, 59, 60, 62–65, 74, 98, 100, 103, 108, 120, 121, 126, 128, 130, 132, 133, 135–137, 142, 154, 156, 157

critique, 13, 14, 78, 81, 82, 104–106, 110, 132, 133, 144, 157

culture of compliance, 11, 54, 92

cybercrime, 33, 65

cybernetic imaginary, 5, 99

D

data-driven, 5, 7–9, 32–35, 41, 50, 51, 63, 64, 92, 98, 100, 115, 116, 119, 123, 125, 126, 133, 135–137, 140, 141, 154, 156

data-driven governance, 99, 136

democracy, 24, 36

deviation, 22

dissent, 78, 81, 100, 106, 110, 157

E

effectivization, 92, 133

emotions, 100, 108, 117, 122, 123, 126, 131, 134, 136, 138

ethical capitalism, 7

ethical compliance, 8, 28, 61

ethical culture, 8, 13, 49, 51, 65, 141

ethics, 7–10, 13, 14, 22, 25, 28, 37, 41, 49, 52, 53, 56, 58, 59, 76, 84, 85, 89, 90, 92, 93, 103, 132, 135, 136, 143, 144, 157

evil, 4, 9, 16, 22, 23, 28, 30, 35, 60

expert, 9, 11, 33, 37, 41, 75–77, 87, 90, 93, 98, 100–105, 110, 111, 116, 119, 130, 132, 134, 142, 144, 155–157

extrastatecraft, 9, 78, 104

F

failure, 16, 36, 85, 101, 108, 110, 125, 142, 157

financial crime, 11, 28–30, 39, 56, 62, 65, 74, 89, 102, 103, 131, 137, 142, 156
fraud, 23, 25, 30, 34, 36, 60, 61, 63, 64, 74, 83, 84, 86, 88, 89, 100, 101, 103, 109, 126, 131, 135, 137, 140, 154, 157
freedom of speech, 78, 82, 136

G
gamification, 126
good governance, 4, 9, 22, 25, 27, 29, 37, 109, 154
governance, 4, 6, 9, 11, 14, 16, 28, 29, 32–39, 47–51, 55, 61–65, 74–78, 91, 93, 98–100, 104, 107–109, 117, 118, 122, 132, 133, 135, 136, 140–143, 153–155
governance of the soul, 58, 93, 135, 136

H
harm, 4, 10, 12, 16, 22, 23, 25, 30, 75, 82, 83, 90, 127, 129, 132, 135, 142, 144
high policing, 89
holistic, 27, 55, 61, 65, 93
human resource management, 92, 97, 137
human rights, 5, 22, 24, 56, 82, 83, 102, 118, 127, 132
hybridization, 35, 55, 60, 61, 77, 91, 153, 155

I
ideological fantasy, 26
injustice, 16, 57, 82, 90, 120, 127, 129, 132, 144

insider threat, 12, 32, 58, 82, 134, 135, 137–139
insider threat management, 60, 65, 93, 125, 135, 137, 141
integrated, 27, 29, 30, 35, 39, 61, 65, 93, 120, 125, 131, 135, 137, 144, 154
integrity, 5, 22, 25, 37, 84, 107, 135, 136, 141
integrity management, 8, 53, 135
intelligence, 5, 6, 9–11, 30–34, 38, 49, 55–60, 63, 64, 74, 85, 91–93, 98, 99, 102, 103, 117, 120, 121, 125–131, 133–138, 144, 153, 155, 156
intelligence-led policing, 57, 99, 118, 125
ISO standards, 12

J
justice, 36, 37, 55, 57, 64, 65, 91, 108, 117, 119, 126, 153

K
knowledge, 9, 12, 24, 37, 55, 75, 76, 78, 85, 92, 98–104, 107, 109, 110, 123, 129, 130, 132–135

L
legalization, 77
legal obligation, 30, 34, 37, 56, 57, 92
low policing, 89

M
management, 5, 7, 10, 11, 27, 33, 53–55, 58, 60–62, 75, 82, 85, 89–91, 93, 98, 102–104, 122, 128, 132, 134–136, 140, 141, 153

management system, 32, 60, 62, 65, 76, 87, 91, 137, 140

money laundering, 8, 28, 34, 39, 65, 103, 131, 154

monitoring, 10, 27, 29, 32, 38, 41, 54, 56, 58, 59, 65, 92, 120–122, 125, 130, 133, 134, 137, 139–141

morality, 25, 28, 34, 50, 56, 109, 110, 153, 157

moral obligation, 6, 30, 37, 56, 58–60, 134

N

national security, 4, 24, 29, 30, 32, 33, 57, 136

neoliberalism, 65

neutrality, 98, 109, 117, 129

nudge, 5, 122

O

objectivity, 50, 98, 110, 115–117, 120, 124, 129

open-source intelligence (OSINT), 32, 60, 103, 130, 139

organized crime, 4, 22, 32, 34, 39, 65, 74, 100, 156

P

philanthrocapitalism, 7

platform, 9, 25, 27, 37, 48, 61, 64, 65, 86, 87, 92, 93, 118, 120, 126, 132, 140, 142, 154

platformization, 93, 102

pluralization of policing, 14, 55

policing, 6, 7, 9, 10, 14, 15, 30–32, 34, 38, 41, 53, 55–57, 59–62, 64, 75, 89, 91, 92, 98, 108, 120–122, 124–128, 130, 132, 134, 136, 140, 141, 144, 153, 155

politics, 5, 25, 27, 31, 60, 77, 117, 120, 144

popular passion, 28

post-political, 144

pre-crime, 5, 6, 41, 55, 90, 99, 100, 120, 122, 130, 133, 134

pre-crime society, 6, 38, 58, 60, 65, 66, 78, 140, 155, 157

prediction, 5, 6, 38, 41, 60, 118, 123, 126, 127, 139

predictive tools, 126

pre-emption, 5, 54

pre-emptive, 30, 31, 41, 54, 75, 76, 91, 92, 120, 121

prevention, 5, 6, 32, 38, 56, 60, 107, 108, 132, 135

preventive state, 75

private intelligence, 33, 35, 41, 56, 58, 60, 117

private security, 14, 60, 74, 75, 120, 121

privatization of policing, 91

professionals, 11, 27, 31, 34, 49, 74, 75, 77, 82, 87, 100, 101, 109, 119, 120, 131, 139, 153, 155, 156

public good, 74, 124

punish, 58, 90, 92, 109, 120

punishment, 6, 29, 75, 125, 136

R

real-time monitoring, 92

RegTech, 6, 11, 32, 33, 41, 48, 54, 60, 63, 64, 92, 93, 102, 111, 130–133, 138, 141–143, 153, 156

regulation, 5, 7, 12, 15, 21, 23, 25, 27–29, 34–36, 39, 40, 47–51, 54–56, 58, 60–63, 74–76, 83, 85, 87, 93, 101, 102, 106, 109,

110, 131–133, 135, 136, 142–144, 153, 154, 156

regulatory blurring, 35

regulatory capitalism, 7, 32, 35, 48, 143, 155

regulatory compliance, 7, 8, 28, 32, 140

regulatory hybridization, 35, 37–39, 76

regulocracy, 10, 110

reputation, 8, 13, 22, 29, 36, 49, 59, 86, 91, 93, 102, 107, 118

reputational risk, 13, 91, 134

risk, 5, 7–9, 11, 16, 23, 25–27, 30, 33, 34, 36, 38, 39, 48, 54–56, 58, 60, 61, 63–65, 75, 82, 83, 87, 90, 92, 93, 98, 101–103, 109, 115–118, 120, 121, 124, 126, 130–133, 135–137, 139–141, 143, 144, 153, 156

risk assessment, 12, 27, 34, 50, 115, 116, 118, 120, 126

risk management, 5, 6, 8, 15, 25, 27, 38, 52, 55, 56, 62, 65, 75, 88, 92, 97, 103, 119, 122, 129, 131, 137, 143

S

sanctions, 7, 29, 32–34, 38, 39, 41, 49, 50, 60, 63, 64, 82, 90–92, 129–131, 134, 135, 142, 153, 154, 156

sanctions regimes, 25, 30, 33, 39, 40, 63

scandal, 22, 36, 38, 49–52, 60, 82, 107

securitization, 5, 7, 9, 14, 28, 37, 38, 40, 61, 65, 93, 108

security, 4–6, 8, 9, 11, 13, 15, 16, 25, 26, 29, 31–33, 38, 55, 56, 58, 59, 61–65, 74, 75, 82, 90,

93, 97–99, 117–126, 128, 129, 133, 134, 136, 140, 141

Social Credit System, 124

sovereignty, 14, 15, 56, 58

special liberty, 157

stakeholder capitalism, 7, 31, 58, 93

standardization, 11, 14, 37, 104–107, 110, 131

state, 6, 7, 11, 13–16, 23, 30–34, 37, 48, 56, 58–60, 63, 74, 75, 84, 86, 91, 93, 123, 125, 129, 130, 134

state authority, 14, 58, 73

strategy, 5, 23, 24, 26, 29–32, 38, 86

surveillance, 8, 10, 27, 30, 32, 38, 49, 51, 55, 56, 58, 61, 63, 65, 83, 92, 103, 110, 117, 118, 120–122, 125, 126, 130, 131, 136, 137, 141, 142, 153, 155

surveillance capitalism, 11, 32, 35, 48, 61, 155

suspicion, 11, 74, 85, 90, 92, 99, 109, 116, 130, 131, 134, 136, 140, 141, 155

suspicious activity reports (SARs), 33, 34, 41, 116, 132

T

technobureaucracy, 16

techno-social engineering, 5, 133

technosolutionism, 37, 51

threat, 4–6, 13, 15, 16, 23–27, 29–31, 33, 34, 36, 38, 39, 50, 54, 56–60, 63–65, 74, 75, 82, 83, 87, 88, 90–92, 100, 101, 120, 124–126, 130, 133–138, 155, 156

transnational crime, 31, 32, 40, 49, 136, 153

transparency, 4, 5, 10, 22, 25, 29, 37, 98, 109, 118, 127, 142, 143, 154, 156

166   INDEX

transversal, 10, 11, 14, 60, 61, 121, 142, 157
transversal social phenomenon, 6

U
uncertainty, 117, 130
uncontrollability, 110
universal, 23, 25, 75, 76, 109

V
values, 9, 22, 28, 37, 49, 53, 89, 93, 107, 116, 132, 135, 136, 139

W
whistleblower, 11, 31, 78, 82–86, 88, 90, 134, 157
whistleblowing, 10, 84–86, 88, 137

Z
zero tolerance, 22, 64, 137